Making Sense of Saints

Fascinating Facts About Relics,
Patrons, Canonization and More

Making Sense of Saints

Fascinating Facts About Relics, Patrons, Canonization and More

Patricia Ann Kasten

Our Sunday Visitor Publishing Division
Our Sunday Visitor, Inc.
Huntington, Indiana 46750

Nihil Obstat:
Msgr. Michael Heintz, Ph.D.
Censor Librorum

Imprimatur:
✠ Kevin C. Rhoades
Bishop of Fort Wayne-South Bend
March 3, 2014

The *Nihil Obstat* and *Imprimatur* are declarations that a work is free from doctrinal or moral error. It is not implied that those who have granted the *Nihil Obstat* and *Imprimatur* agree with the contents, opinions, or statements expressed.

ISBN 978-1-61278-742-8 (Inventory No. T1553)
eISBN: 978-1-61278-344-4
LCCN: 2014934367

Cover design: Lindsey Riesen
Cover art: Shutterstock

PRINTED IN THE UNITED STATES OF AMERICA

Contents

Introduction

They've surrounded us all our lives. Standing in the corners of our churches. Adorning medals pinned to our clothing. On prayer cards given to us at funerals. They even stand on our automobile dashboards.

They're the saints. We all know who they are, at least we know the big names: Paul, Peter, Patrick, and even Perpetua. But how did they get there? How did they get to become saints, people of holy example in our popular awareness?

In other words, what makes a saint a saint?

Officially, that's varied over the centuries. In the beginning years of the Christian Church, it was pretty clear to everyone who the saints were: those who had been Christ's disciples, his friends and his family. After they had died, there were the disciples of the Apostles, and the martyrs who had given their lives for love of Jesus and of his Gospel.

However, the centuries continued to pass and the Church spread around a world that did not have the benefits of today's global news media and instant social communication. People who were considered saints in one place were totally unknown anywhere else. Oh, there were stories, spread by travelers and wandering pilgrims who brought news of a new saint. Yet their words weren't always reliable and questions could arise.

To deal with those questions and to protect the overly trusting, the structure of canonization was developed by the Church. Canonization was never about "naming saints," as some might think, but about declaring that a particular person had lived a holy life in imitation of Christ and that this person was now alive with Christ in heaven.

Yet, for each of us, questions still remain: What is a saint? How does one become a saint? And, more importantly, why do the saints matter to me? How do they touch me, in my own life today, right here, right now, whatever my struggles and hopes are? Might I even know a real live saint, or at least people who seem to live lives that might be considered saint-like?

Finally, how do the saints help me to live that sort of life, the life of a saint? Right here, right now? How can I not only know about the saints, but how can I start to live a life that is, in some small way, "Sainthood now?"

CHAPTER ONE

Santo Subito —
"Sainthood Now!"

"What do we want?"

"Sainthood."

"When do we want it?"

"Now!"

In late March 2005, as Pope John Paul II lay dying, thousands gathered in St. Peter's Square outside the papal apartments in Vatican City. They prayed. They waited. And when he died on April 2, they held up signs proclaiming "*Santo subito*," meaning "a saint at once (immediately)," or more colloquially, "sainthood now" in Italian.

It may have reminded those watching of banners from the 1960s and 1970s of "Peace Now" and "Make Love, Not War." But, unlike the protest generations of the late twentieth century, these well-wishers were reflecting an ages-old tradition in the Church: making saints by popular declaration.

While the process of canonization — the formal recognition of saints — is now a lengthy process overseen by the Vatican's Congregation for the Causes of Saints, such was not always the case. In fact, the first recorded canonization by a pope was not until the tenth century when Pope John XV canonized St. Ulrich of Augsburg in 993. It took another couple of centuries until Pope Gregory IX, in 1234, ordered the process of canonization placed under the auspices of the Bishop of Rome so that no one could be called a saint unless the pope had declared him or her as such. Another few centuries passed. Then, in 1588, Pope Sixtus V founded the Sacred Congregation for Rites, now called the Congregation for the Causes of Saints.

Prior to that, sainthood was determined much more informally and most often began with a popular outcry — known as *vox populi* or "the voice of the people" in Latin. The entire phrase is *"Vox populi; Vox Dei"* ("The voice of the people is the voice of God"). No banners, perhaps, and certainly no megaphones, but the idea was the same: popular outcry. People first heard about the goodness of a holy person while he or she was alive and came to hear him or her speak. When these holy persons died, people came to their graves to pray and, yes, to seek miracles. Many miracles did take place and the common people, on their own, came to speak of these people as saints. Of course, this worked well for everyone: word spread in its own time, which gave plenty of time for any claims of miracles to be explored and studied, at least informally, by Church leaders.

As Jesuit Fr. Paul Molinari explained, "In the first centuries, the popular fame or the *vox populi* represented in practice the only criterion by which a person's holiness was ascertained. A new element was gradually introduced, namely, the intervention of the ecclesiastical authority, i.e., of the competent bishop. However, the fame of sanctity, as a result of which the faithful piously visited the person's tomb, invoked his intercession, and proclaimed the thaumaturgic (miraculous) effects of it, remained the starting point of those inquiries that culminated with a definite pronouncement on the part of the bishop." [1]

This "fame of sanctity," springing up from the grass roots, has always been taken as a sign of God's presence, of the Holy Spirit moving through and working in the Church. The wisdom of the Church has always watched for signs of the Holy Spirit's movement amongst the people of God. We can see this even from the very beginnings of the Church, when Peter and the other Apostles, led by the Holy Spirit, preached in Jerusalem. When the Sanhedrin had Peter and the others brought before them to forbid them to teach about Jesus, they replied, "We are witnesses of these things, as is the Holy Spirit that God has given to those who obey him" (Acts 5:32).

The Jewish leaders, of course, were enraged and would have ordered Peter and his companions executed, had not one of their own number, the Rabbi Gamaliel (who had taught Paul in his youth and who was greatly respected by the people) stopped them. "'Fellow Israelites, be careful what you are about to do to these men…. For if this endeavor or this activity is of human origin, it will destroy itself. But if it comes from God, you will not be able to destroy them; you may even find yourselves fighting against God.' They were persuaded by him" (Acts 5:35–39).

Clearly, Gamaliel, while not a Christian himself, understood that God spoke through both religious leaders and through the common people. In much the same way, the Church continues to discern whether or not a popular person has saintly qualities.

In college, I took some criminology classes alongside many active police personnel. In learning investigation procedure, we were taught that, if there are ten witnesses to a crime, there will be ten different stories about the same event. A criminal lawyer will tell you much the same thing. This is why the justice system cannot accept the word of any one of these ten witnesses in isolation. What is needed to get to the truth is to look at the story that comes together from piecing the entire group's many different viewpoints into one whole. That's why a jury trial is used in criminal cases, because the sense of the group, the common sense of "the common man," when they look at the evidence and hear the stories of many witnesses, reveals the truth. This truth shows itself consistently, even through the varied descriptions of any one event.

The same process that works in jury trials works when we examine the jury of the people of God and what the Church calls the *sensus fidei fidelium* or the "sense of the faith of the faithful." This complex Latin term basically means that we believe that the Church, collectively speaking as the People of God, cannot err because it is guided by the Holy Spirit. When we take the stories of many people, revealed through the Spirit, and look at them as a whole, we will see the Will of God revealed. The more commonly used — and shorter — term is *sensus fidelium* (the sense of the faithful). The Bishops of the Second Vatican Council, in their Dogmatic Constitution on the Church, *Lumen Gentium*, explained this sense of the faithful:

> The holy people of God shares also in Christ's prophetic office; it spreads abroad a living witness to Him, especially by means of a life of faith and charity and by offering to God a sacrifice of praise, the tribute of lips which give praise to His name. The entire body of the faithful, anointed as they are by the Holy One, cannot err in matters of belief.... That discernment in matters of faith is aroused and sustained by the Spirit of Truth.... Through it, the people of God adheres unwaveringly to the faith given once and for all to the saints, penetrates it more deeply with right thinking, and applies it more fully in its life. (No. 12)

During the first 1,200 years of the Church, this "sense of the faithful" guided the selection of recognized saints. From the Apostles who had walked with Jesus to saints like St. Francis of Assisi, who died in 1226 and was canonized in 1228 by Pope Gregory IX (because of Francis' great popularity), common everyday people have been drawn to holy men and women, sought their guidance and blessings, and visited their tombs after their deaths. Why? Because they believed that, even in death, these holy people could help them because "they were with God." In the minds of the faithful, they had *Santo subito*, Sainthood now.

There are approximately 7,000 saints in "The Roman Martyrology," the official but not exhaustive list of the saints of the Catholic Church. The Martyrology was first compiled in 1583 and was last extensively revised in 2001 (with another editorial update in 2004). Most of the saints and blesseds on the list today were also there before Pope Gregory IX in 1234. In fact, since Gregory's day, only about 1,800 names have been officially added, including the 482 canonized by Pope John Paul II between 1978 and 2005. During his eight years on the Chair of Peter, Pope Benedict XVI added another 45 canonized saints to the list. Of course, the numbers increased greatly in 2013, and a record was probably set, when Pope Francis canonized the 800 Martyrs of Otranto (Italy) on May 12, 2013. (He also canonized Laura di Santa Caterina da Siena Montoya y Upegui and Maria Guadalupe García Zavala that day.)

The process of canonization takes years. The formal investigation into the sanctity of a proposed saint's life may only begin after five years pass following his or her death. However, papal exceptions can be made. Pope John Paul II did just that after Mother Teresa of Calcutta died on September 5, 1997. He opened her sainthood cause in 1999, and she was declared blessed (beatified) on October 19, 2003. (In turn, Pope Benedict XVI did the same for his predecessor, waiving the five-year waiting period completely and opening John Paul II's sainthood cause on May 13, 2005, less than six weeks after the late pope's death.)

The speed of the sainthood process for the founder of the Missionaries of Charity was aided by the fact that, even during her life, Mother Teresa was called "a living saint." From the late 1960s, when she first came to public attention for her work with the poor in Calcutta, until her death there in 1997, people across the social spectrum came to view her as a holy person;

from Pope John Paul II to Princess Diana, she was admired and emulated. As early as December 29, 1975, when *Time* Magazine ran a cover story on her, we can see the secular media calling her a living saint. In one way or another, they echoed the words of Thomas Malcolm Muggeridge, the late British author and media personality. [2]

Muggeridge did much to bring Mother Teresa to the world's attention. He even became a Catholic at age 79, largely, he said, due to the influence of Blessed Mother Teresa. Muggeridge had filmed a documentary about her in 1969, "Something Beautiful for God," for BBC and later compiled his experiences into a book by the same title (1971). In it, he said of Mother Teresa:

> Pretty well everyone who has met her will agree, I think, that she is a unique person in the world today; not in our vulgar celebrity sense of having neon lighting about her head. Rather in the opposite sense — of someone who has merged herself in the common face of mankind, and identified herself with human suffering and privation. [3]

When Mother Teresa was beatified in 2003, Pope John Paul II addressed the pilgrims who had gathered in Vatican Square for the event. He called Mother Teresa a true missionary, which he defined as: "A missionary with the most universal language: the language of love that knows no bounds or exclusion and has no preferences other than for the most forsaken." [4]

This is how the sense of the faithful is triggered by someone like Mother Teresa or, indeed, by the life of any saint throughout church history: through a universal language that reveals a love that is beyond human dimensions. Examples abound.

The first century's **Lydia of Thyatira**, mentioned as a convert in Acts 16. Lydia opened her home as a house church for Christians in her town. In the Eastern Orthodox churches, St.

Lydia is called Lydia of Philippia and is known as "Equal to the Apostles," because she led many throughout the region to embrace Christianity.

The fourth century bishop, **Nicholas of Myra**, revered by both Eastern and Western Catholics, as well as many Protestants. Known for his care for the poor and for children, as well as being a beloved patron of sailors, St. Nicholas became the seed for many Christmastime traditions.

The twelfth century's **Hildegard of Bingen**, a Benedictine abbess, writer, herbalist, musical composer, and mystic. Hildegard was so popular that she was beatified soon after her death in 1179, and her feast day was informally added to the Church's calendar. On May 10, 2012, Pope Benedict XVI formally extended her feast day to the entire church, an act that is equivalent to formal canonization.

The beloved nineteenth-century **Curé d'Ars, St. Jean-Baptiste Marie Vianney**. This humble French priest was not a scholar and not really even a very learned priest. In fact, because he had barely been able to complete seminary training and had proved to be, at best, only an adequate homilist, Fr. Vianney was sent to the outskirts of his diocese, to Ars-sur-Formans, a town of 230 people. However, there he proved to be a phenomenal confessor and was credited with the spiritual gift of being able to read souls. His popularity grew and people soon came from all over to gain his guidance. He was so famous, in fact, that the French government needed to add a railway spur from Lyon to Ars to accommodate the estimated 20,000 people who visited the Curé each year. Toward the end of his life, Fr. Vianney could be found in his confessional for 12 to 18 hours a day so that he could accommodate all who came. He died in 1859 and was declared "Venerable" 15 years later.

Also in the nineteenth century is **Fr. Damien de Veuster**, who arrived in Honolulu in 1864 for a missionary life that would end with his own death from leprosy in 1889. In 1873, he volunteered to serve as priest for the 816 lepers living in exile on the island of Molokai. He arrived to find a Wild West of a settlement, with drunkenness, prostitution, and despair ruling the lives of the sick people there. From then until his death, Fr. Damien became the driving force that transformed the town of Kalaupapa into a Christian community, even helping to enlarge the Church of St. Philomena with his own hands. Fr. Damien also built furniture, dug graves, and ministered to the sick even after he became ill himself. When he learned he had contracted leprosy in 1884, the priest announced his condition to his congregation at Mass by opening the celebration not with his customary "Brethren," but with the words: "We lepers." When he died, the entire community followed him to his grave. By an act of the Hawaii State Legislature, every April 15 — the day he died — is Fr. Damien Day in the Aloha State. On that day, his statue, which stands at the entrance of the state capitol in Honolulu, is draped with flower leis. Even Mahatma Gandhi heard of and admired Fr. Damien, saying of him, "The political and journalistic world can boast of very few heroes who compare with Fr. Damien of Molokai." [5] Pope Benedict XVI canonized Fr. Damien on Oct. 11, 2009.

Another of those "thousands" who devoted themselves to those with leprosy was **Mother Marianne Cope**, who arrived in the Hawaiian Islands in 1883. Five years later, she went to Molokai to assist Fr. Damien during his final illness. She assumed many of the Belgian priest's duties and remained at the leper colony until her own death in 1918. She was approved for beatification by Pope John Paul II in 2004 and the ceremony took place on May 14, 2005, the first beatification Mass celebrated by Pope Benedict XVI. She was canonized on October 21, 2012.

And it was Pope Benedict, following the *sensus fidelium* of those crowds in St. Peter's Square and countless other voices around the world, who referred to his predecessor as "**John Paul the Great**" at the late pontiff's Mass of Repose on April 3, 2005. Only three other popes in the history of the Church have received the title of "the great." There is no formal process for bestowing this appellation; instead it arises from popular custom. It was also Pope Benedict XVI who, on his own papal authority and citing the extraordinary circumstances such as the *Santo subito* proclamations, bypassed the five-year waiting period for opening the sainthood cause for his predecessor. On May 13, 2005, the cause for John Paul II was opened in the Diocese of Rome, of which Benedict was the bishop. (A sainthood cause is formally opened by the bishop of the diocese in which the deceased lived or worked.) Pope John Paul II was beatified on May 1, 2011. At that time, his body was exhumed from its original tomb in the papal grottoes — where it had received up to 12,000 visitors a day, many leaving prayers and touching rosaries to the site — and moved. It now rests in a chapel on the main floor of the St. Peter's Basilica. Not only does this site better accommodate the crowds of visitors wanting to see that late pope's tomb, but it is also near one of the most famous works of art depicting the Mother of God to whom Pope John Paul was so devoted: the Pietà.

When John Paul's May 1, 2011, beatification took place, thousands lined the streets around St. Peter's Basilica, waiting throughout the night, even though they knew that they would never get close enough to see anything of the ceremony. Just being there was enough for these faithful. One person there that night was a young student studying at the Pontifical Lateran University in Rome. Later, she told the news media what John Paul II had meant in her life:

> "Pope John Paul II was the hero of my high school years. At the time when I was preparing for confirmation, I took

a serious look at saints who could be my role model, and there was no one else like him: lover of nature, of theatre, and of man, not afraid to follow his conscience in the face of danger, not afraid to practice rugged purity in love." [6]

Being a hero may not be the first image we think of when we think of saints — after all, heroes do things like leap into flaming buildings to recue people — but the heroism of saints from Peter to Fr. Damien to John Paul II has touched the hearts of people like this student in St. Peter's Square and stirred the fire of the Holy Spirit within them. That is the sense of the faithful that stirs people to cry, "*Santo subito.*" It can be stirred to life in a moment, or gradually build up through centuries.

As the well-remembered television personality, Archbishop Fulton J. Sheen — whose cause for sainthood led to his declaration as Venerable on June 28, 2012 — reminded us: it isn't about time, but about love. "For it does not require much time to make us saints," he wrote, "it requires only much love." [7]

Discussion/Reflection:

1. Who is the first saint that you remember being aware of? What about him or her, what "fame of sanctity," caught your attention?

2. Do you know someone, living in this world or in the next, for whom you would want to wave the banner of "*Santo subito?*"

3. Of the saints listed in this chapter, what character traits do they all seem to share?

CHAPTER TWO

"Holy Halos, God-Made-Man!"

Saints and Martyrs as Superheroes

"We know them when we see them." With a nod to the late U.S. Supreme Court Justice Potter Stewart, who issued that slightly different but more famous 1964 statement regarding pornography (a bad thing), what we know from the ancient traditions of the Church to this day is that the average person knows a saint (a good thing) when he or she sees one.

Certainly the first recognized saints were those who were closest to Jesus: His family (His mother, Mary; His father, Joseph; His cousin, John); His friends (Martha and Mary of Bethany, Mary Magdalene, Joseph of Arimathea); and His closest companions (the Twelve, including the late-named Matthias).

After Jesus' resurrection, the Good News was spread by these people and, as more people heard about Jesus and came to believe He was the Christ, they also came to believe in the holiness of these close companions of Jesus. We can see this in the records of the Acts of the Apostles: "but the people esteemed them…. Thus they even carried the sick out into the streets and laid them on cots and mats so that when Peter came by, at least his shadow might fall on one or another of them" (5:13–15).

The Apostles and the other disciples were regarded as good and holy people, which is basically our definition of a saint. Our English word "saint" derives from a French word *seinte*, which in turn comes from the Latin *sanctus* for "holy" and the Latin verb *sancire* for "consecrated." The original Greek word — since the first written language of the Gospels was Greek — is *hagios*, a word used to identify holy and sacred things.

Even before this first generation of the Church's holy ones began to die, other Christians came to be recognized as "holy." For example, in the Acts of the Apostles, we see Tabitha (also known by her Greek name of Dorcas) living in Joppa. Joppa (now called Jaffa) is in the most ancient part of the modern city of Tel Aviv. Tabitha is called "a disciple" in Acts 9, and we see that she "was completely occupied with good deeds and almsgiving" (9:36). When she fell so ill that she died, the disciples and local widows in Joppa sought out Peter, who was in the city at the time. They brought him to Tabitha's deathbed, "weeping and showing him the tunics and cloaks that Dorcas had made while she was with them" (9:39). Peter prayed over Tabitha and, by the grace of God, she was restored to life — and, no doubt, to her good works.

While the Apostles, Jesus' family, and people like Tabitha were long recognized as models of holiness, the first formal "saints of the Church" were the martyrs. They were the ones who imitated Christ — to the point of giving their lives rather than denouncing their faith. They became models for others, especially as the fledging Church faced persecution.

Returning to the Acts of the Apostles, but before Tabitha's story, we find Stephen, one of the first seven deacons of the Church. Today, we know Stephen as the Proto-martyr, or "first martyr," for the faith (Acts 7). Stephen was a wonderful preacher and boldly proclaimed the Gospel. In doing so, though, he angered the Jewish religious leaders who felt that his interpretation of the Scriptures was blasphemy. They had him stoned, and Stephen, as he was about to die, made his last proclamation: he echoed the words of Jesus on the Cross and forgave his murderers. This only increased his sanctity in the eyes of early Christians.

Stephen and others like him drew the Church together. At first, celebrations of the Eucharist were held in house churches. But as the Church grew and began to come under attack, celebrations of the Mass took place elsewhere. Most often, this was over the graves of these martyrs, with altars being erected right over their tombs. The early Church firmly believed that these heroic and faithful people had lived as Christ had lived and had died in faithful witness to him. The Church believed that these martyrs were now saints with God and, as Stephen had testified as he died, beheld the glory of God in heaven. So their graves became hallowed ground, places where people felt somehow closer to God.

The word "martyr" comes from the Greek *martus*, meaning "witness." Originally, the term referred to the Apostles, who had witnessed the events of Jesus' life — and also died for the faith (except St. John). However, as more early Christians died for the faith, "martyr" soon came to mean anyone who, while not seeing or hearing the human Jesus, so firmly believed in Him that they were willing to sacrifice their lives to witness to His Gospel. As the *Catechism of the Catholic Church* notes about martyrs: "Martyrdom is the supreme witness given to the truth of the faith.... The martyr bears witness to Christ who died and rose, to whom he is united by charity" (CCC 2473).

Martyrs strove to be like Jesus, forgiving those who killed them, bolstering the faith of those who accompanied them to death, and exhorting those who would follow after them. One only needs to remember the example of the third-century Christian martyrs Perpetua and Felicity, who went to their deaths lovingly supporting each other, to see how martyrs offer strength to others.

After the Apostles and martyrs, the early Church wide-
ly acclaimed as saints those whom we now call the confessors,
also known as "confessors of the faith." These were those early
Church leaders who suffered for the faith in various ways, but
who had not been killed and thus did not merit the crown of
martyrdom. St. Paul, himself a martyr, gives an excellent de-
scription of what a "confessor" might endure in his Second Letter to the Corinthians: "Five times at the hands of the Jews I
received forty lashes minus one. Three times I was beaten with
rods, once I was stoned, three times I was shipwrecked; I passed
a night and a day on the deep; on frequent journeys, in dangers
from rivers, dangers from robbers, dangers from my own race,
dangers from Gentiles, dangers in the city, dangers in the wilder-
ness, dangers at sea, dangers among false brothers; in toil and
hardship, through many sleepless nights, through hunger and
thirst, through frequent fastings, through cold and exposure"
(11:24–27).

If Paul hadn't died a martyr, he would certainly have been
remembered as a confessor. "Confessor" comes from the Latin
word *confiteor,* for "profession." Today, we use the same word for
the prayer we use at the opening of Mass by which we confess
our sins and profess our belief in God's mercy. The confessors
lived out this profession.

The Catholic Encyclopedia defines "confessor" as "a title of
honor (used) to designate those brave champions of the Faith
who had confessed Christ publicly in time of persecution and
had been punished with imprisonment, torture, exile, or labor
in the mines, remaining faithful in their confession until the
end of their lives. The title thus distinguished them from the
martyrs, who were so called because they underwent death for
the Faith." [8]

St. John the Evangelist is honored as one of the Twelve
Apostles, but he could also be considered a confessor. He was

the only Apostle who did not die a martyr's death. Not that the opponents of the Christian faith didn't try to kill John. Early Christian writers such as Tertullian record that John suffered greatly, even being thrown into a cauldron of boiling oil during the persecution of Christians under the Roman emperor Domitian. However, John emerged from the caldron unscathed. Legend also says he was saved from drinking poisoned wine. Clearly John suffered for the faith — not only by oil and poison, but also through enduring exile and prison.

One would hardly belittle John's trials, or those of countless others who patiently endured as he did. So the term "confessor" is used for saints who were clearly heroes in their own right and all but companions of the martyrs — since they gave witness with their lives. Some of the earliest recognized confessors were the third-century abbot St. Anthony of Egypt, also called the Father of Monks, and his protégé St. Hilarion, both of whom chose to live in solitude in the deserts in order to seek God with undivided attention. Both experienced great interior struggles with spiritual dryness, while they physically endured the outer dryness of Egypt and Palestine. But their perseverance drew many to come to learn from them and to find Christ.

Confessors are not just part of ancient tradition; they have remained with us throughout Church history. In the Western Church, the title of confessor was most often given to those of the second and third generations of the Church, such as the Desert Fathers and Mothers. However, the 1917 *Code of Canon Law* still referred to anyone who was to be canonized as "martyrs, virgins, or confessors." And many continued to receive that formal title in later centuries. From the fourth-century bishop Paul of Constantinople to the eleventh-century St. Edward the Confessor — the last Anglo-Saxon king of England — the Church has bestowed this formal title on saints who were brave enough to be willing to give their lives if necessary for Christ's church.

To this day, the Eastern Orthodox churches recognize saints by the title of "confessor." For example, in 1996, the Russian Orthodox Church recognized St. Luke (born Valentin Felixovich Voino-Yasenetsky), an archbishop of Crimea who was also a renowned surgeon, as a confessor. "Holy Hiero-Confessor St. Luke" is honored with a June 11 feast day. He was a fierce defender of the Christian faith who spent many years in prison, and was even exiled to Siberia because of his opposition to the Soviet government. He certainly earned the title of hero as well as any of the early martyrs.

Just like the heroes of the early Church, we also seek to live our lives in ways that witness to and confess the Lord Jesus. At each Mass, we pray the Confiteor and acknowledge our need for God's mercy. Later in the Mass, in the Creed (the Profession of Faith), we voice aloud our belief and steadfast faith as disciples of Christ. Privately and in shared prayers like the Rosary, we pray the Apostles Creed, credited to the earliest disciples. All of these professions remind us of our desire to live as heroes for Christ and to boldly proclaim our identities as His disciples.

When I was a child, I thought that having a secret identity would be very cool. You know, like Clark Kent's secret identity as Superman and Bruce Wayne's as Batman. Not only did they have secret identities, they were secret heroes who could do all sorts of cool things: fly or walk through walls or have super vision. At the very least, they had secret agent gadgets that they could use to save the world from disaster.

Well, surprise! It turns out that I *am* a secret agent. You are too. We are special agents, superheroes with a special identity: we are disciples of Christ. And we stand in a long line of hero disciples, from the Apostles to the confessors of modern day, all of whom lived as superheroes and special agents for Christ. In fact, in a special and very true sense, you and I *are* Christ because Christ is *in* you and me. His power is revealed in us, through the Holy

Spirit. Jesus Christ, Emmanuel, "Holy God-Made-Man" himself, is right there with us, feeding us with His Body and Blood and remaking us into His own image. Just as He was right there helping all his martyrs and confessors, forming them into His special agents, His superheroes, He does the same for us today.

St. Paul said this very thing in his Second Letter to the Corinthians: "So we are ambassadors for Christ, as if God were appealing through us" (2 Cor 5:20). (I think it's okay to read "ambassadors for Christ" as "secret agents for Christ.")

God wants us to be like His only begotten Son — the Holy God-Made-Man — living out His mission to reveal God's love to the whole world. To do this, we have been given God's own Spirit to guide us to be more and more like Christ. That same Spirit, Who anointed Christ at His baptism, continues to entrust the saints — God's holy and special agents — with Christ's not-so-secret mission: to proclaim the Good News of salvation.

The *Catechism of the Catholic Church* reminds us that God adopted us, chose us, and, by Baptism, "makes us other 'christs'" (CCC 2782). "Christ" comes from a Greek word meaning "anointed." In ancient Israel, only the king — who was also called "God's son" — was anointed with oil. Our own anointing at Baptism puts the mark of the Holy Spirit's seal upon us and symbolizes the abundance of God's holiness that fills us in the sacrament. That abundance of God's Spirit gives us the (secret agent/superhero) power to be disciples, just as it did for the early martyrs and confessors.

We are meant to be Jesus' special agents, God's anointed ones, working for the Kingdom of God (okay, you can call it His Majesty's Secret Service), giving service to others.

As the Fathers of Vatican II told us, "All Christians by the example of their lives and the witness of the word, wherever they live, have an obligation to manifest the new man which they put on in Baptism, and to reveal the power of the Holy Spirit" (*Ad Gentes*, Decree on Missionary Activity in the Church, No. 11).

As Jesus' special agents, how do we know we are fulfilling this obligation, this mission? Dennis Sweetland, a theologian at Saint Anselm College in New Hampshire, offered the following checklist to identify disciples. It also works pretty well to expose the secret identity of any special agent of Christ: [9]

- Commitment to the person and work of Jesus;
- Severing of old ties to embrace the new family of Jesus, the Church;
- A life of mutual service;
- A turning away from power and prestige;
- Willingness to suffer injustice rather than inflict it on others;
- Trust in God even in the face of suffering and death;
- Fulfilling the role of missionary and joyfully proclaiming the message of salvation.

It's a big list. And if it doesn't take the powers of a super-hero, I don't know what does. But remember, we have the powers of the greatest of all superheroes to call upon: God-Made-Man himself. Other saints, from Paul to Mother Teresa, drew on that power. We can do the same.

One last thing about secret agents. They always have special codes. We do too. Ours is the Gospel. In it, we find messages about the Kingdom and how to reveal it to the world. The *Catechism of the Catholic Church* tells us that these messages are especially apparent in the parables.

> Through his parables, (Jesus) invites people to the feast of the kingdom, but he also asks for radical choice: to gain the kingdom, one must give everything.... Jesus and the

presence of the kingdom in this world are secretly at the heart of the parables. One must enter the kingdom, that is, become a disciple of Christ, in order to "know the secret of the kingdom of heaven" (Mt 13:11). For those who stay "outside," everything remains enigmatic. (CCC 546)

Our code book, unlike the code books of secret agents, is not really a secret. It might seem "enigmatic," but it is meant for everyone. The Gospels are an open invitation to all and Christ sends us as his special agents to share that invitation with the whole world. If it requires us to be superheroes — even to the point of death — then we'll be given exactly what we need to face even that.

Discussion/Reflection:

1. Do you have a favorite super hero? Think about their super abilities. How would those abilities translate into the super abilities of a Christian?

2. Think about people you know of who are heroes. What made them heroic? Did it take an element of faith?

3. Has there ever been a time when you have been a witness for your faith? What gave you courage, or at least the ability to "hang in there"?

4. Look at the traits of a disciple of Christ above. Which trait is the most difficult for you?

CHAPTER THREE

With Only a Pole to Stand On

The Early Monastics

It's lonely in the desert. When I was about eight, my family took a road trip out West. Somewhere in the desert of New Mexico, we got a flat tire. It was late in the evening. My little brother and I had to sit on suitcases beside the road while Dad jacked up the car and put on the spare. It seemed to take a long time, with the sun going down on a bleak landscape. No other cars came along. Dust blew over the road. It was very quiet.

Suppertime consisted of a can of spaghetti pried open with a bottle opener and eaten cold. I began to worry about the coming nightfall. I could tell Mom was nervous too. We saw vultures wheeling overhead, and I was reminded of cartoons and coyotes.

Dad finally got the tire fixed and we headed into the approaching night. Hours later, we came over a dark hillcrest and saw the lights of Albuquerque spread out below. Finally the night didn't feel so lonely.

Every religious man and woman, in some fashion, traces his or her way of life to the deserts of the Middle East. Monasticism — which technically means "to live alone" — is a broad term commonly used to refer to members of religious communities who live quietly in a religious community, of some form or other, with the goal of achieving sacred union with God. While not every religious order would call itself "monastic," each religious order traces its way of life back to the Desert Fathers and Mothers (such as St. Jerome and St. Mary of Egypt).

After the time of the Apostles, the Church moved into the Apostolic Age (which began in the second century). This age began with the students of the Apostles, many of whom became martyrs themselves while others were the first Confessors. Many others of these early saints of the Church came to be referred to as the "Desert Fathers" (*and* Mothers). As the title implies, they often took what they had learned from the Apostles, or from the disciples of the Apostles, and took that knowledge with them into the deserts of the Middle East. From them, we received not only the example of super heroes, but also the origins of Christian monastic life.

Desert theology is at the root of monastic life. Its basic practices were refined into a clear pattern by Christians of the third and fourth centuries. One of the best known, and the model for many after him, was St. Anthony of Egypt (b. A.D. 251). He is called "the Father of Monasticism," even though his desert way of life was practiced by many others even during his lifetime. Desert theology followed the ideal of withdrawal from the world — loosely imitating the history of Old Testament prophets like Elijah and even the wanderings of the Israelites in the desert. However, unlike the prophets and the wandering Hebrew people, there is an added element to this way of life: a hermit. (John the Baptist, while living in a similar fashion, is not a model for this desert way of life because, while he was a prophet and lived in the desert areas, his public ministry disqualifies him from being called a hermit.)

Desert Fathers like Anthony and St. Pachomius (b. A.D. 292) chose to withdraw from worldly life. The word "hermit" comes to us from the Greek words *eremia*, meaning "desert," and *eremos*, meaning "solitary." A true hermit not only lived in the desert, but chose a solitary way of life in order to draw closer to God.

St. Athanasius, Anthony's pupil and biographer, noted that the desert hermits sought to imitate Christ's life of poverty, obedience, and chastity. To learn from Jesus, they chose to "follow Him" (as Jesus asked in the Gospel) by going out into the desert as Jesus Himself had done before the start of His own public ministry. Anthony first lived as an ascetic.

An ascetic is not a true hermit, but one who lives near cities, in simple poverty and solitude, praying and supporting himself in small ways, often by handicrafts. Eventually, Anthony wanted even more solitude than he could find near his home town of Koma in lower Egypt, so he withdrew further into the desert. For a time, he even lived in a tomb. However, after many years, people still talked about him and his spiritual life, and they sought him out for guidance. Soon, small communities developed around Anthony, and other monastics came who chose to live like him. These communities — and others like them — basically evolved into two types:

- The eremitics — individual hermits living in their own small huts, but grouped near each other and, often, sharing a chapel for Mass;

- The cenobitics — those who lived together in community all the time. *Cenobitic* comes from two Greek words: *koine* (common) and *bios* for (life).

Anthony lived a long time in the desert, dying in A.D. 356 at the age of 104. Around A.D. 360, St. Athanasius wrote the *Life of Antony*, and this biography became the model for Eastern monasticism.

St. Pachomius, who is called the "Father of Cenobitic monasticism," was one of those who followed the early hermits into the desert. He learned the eremitical lifestyle under the guidance of a hermit named Palemon, who took him into his own cell as a disciple. Pachomius, who is sometimes called Pachomius the Great, later founded his first monastery at Tebennisi on an island in the Nile River. Before he died in 346, Pachomius had founded several large monasteries for men and two for women.

The lifestyle of the hermits and, indeed of many early monastics, is collectively called asceticism. Ascetics followed a lifestyle that was not unique to Christians, even though it shares many characteristics of the styles of St. Paul, John the Baptist, and even Jesus Himself. Instead, asceticism springs from Greek history and originally referred to a regimen, or form of exercise, often practiced by soldiers or athletes. Ascetics disciplined their bodies for various reasons. Remember the Spartan warriors when you think of Greek ascetics. Christian ascetics disciplined themselves, not for sports or warfare, but in order to imitate Christ who had denied himself the joys and glories of heaven to win the salvation of humanity. Christian ascetics denied themselves many things in order to avoid attachment to the world, to practice humility, and also to atone for sins — both their own and the sins of others.

St. Paul alluded to this way of life in his First Letter to the Corinthians: "Every athlete exercises discipline in every way. They do it to win a perishable crown, but we [for] an imperishable one. Thus I do not run aimlessly; I do not fight as if I were shadowboxing. No, I drive my body and train it, for fear that, after having preached to others, I myself should be disqualified" (9:25–27).

Not all ascetics lived in the same way. Some lived alone, some lived in small groups. One of the more colorful of these ascetic Christian lifestyles was that of the Stylites. Stylites get their name from the Greek word for "pillar" (*stylos*). These people — most were men, but there appear to have been women stylites as well — lived on top of pillars, lost in prayer and the contemplation of God. Instead of retreating to the desert, they took to the sky.

Most sources agree that the first of these pillar saints was St. Simeon Stylites the Elder. This fifth-century saint is recognized not only in the Latin-rite church, but also in Eastern Orthodox churches, Eastern Catholic churches, and the Coptic Catholic Church. In the West, his feast is celebrated on January 5. For thirty-seven years — he lived to be 70 — Simeon lived on top of various pillars in Syria, near the modern city of Aleppo. The last of his pillars was at least fifty-five feet tall. (Some Eastern sources claim it was eighty feet tall.) The pillar was about three feet square and Simeon stood upon it, day in and day out. Eventually, a sort of wall was built around him to help him stay upright, but he was constantly exposed to the elements.

While Simeon — and other stylites such as St. Luke the Younger (d. 953) and St. Daniel the Stylite (d. 493) — lived on a pillar, he actually was not isolated from others. A ladder was kept nearby so that people could climb up beside him to seek counsel. He would also preach from his pillar and wrote letters to various people, including St. Genevieve in Paris. Simeon even counseled the Byzantine Emperors Theodosius II and Leo I.

People sought Simeon's advice because they hoped that he could direct them on how to live a better Christian life. Since he, like other ascetic saints, was not focused on the things of this world, people sensed that Simeon was not as easily trapped by the worries of this world. Thus they felt that he could more clearly see what was important for gaining eternal life.

In the West, ascetic saints like Jerome (d. 420) and Martin of Tours (316–397) became early models for monastic life in Europe. (They did not live on pillars, but Jerome did die in a hermit's cell outside of Bethlehem, where he had lived for 34 years.) Martin had been a cavalry officer in the Roman army, but left to become a Christian hermit. He eventually gathered a small community around him in Ligugé, which became the first monastery in Gaul (later France). Even after Martin was named Bishop of Tours in 371, he continued to practice his monastic style of life.

These early communities eventually developed ways of life that translated into the guidelines for monastic communities that continue to this day. In 1998, I became a leader of one of countless parish-based faith-sharing groups of people preparing for the millennial year. In our diocese, we used material developed by RENEW International, begun in 1976 to follow the renewal of the Church called for by the Second Vatican Council. Each month, our group followed study guides that were divided into five parts emphasizing "five essential signs of communal life: sharing, learning, mutual support, mission, and prayers. These elements express a spirituality that acknowledges complete dependence upon God for the creation of community." [10]

Whenever we gathered, our faith-sharing group (which continued to meet for seven years) prayed together, learned together, supported each other, shared our stories, and committed ourselves to live out the Gospel mission until we met again. Each of the five elements we used as guides, of course, came from Church traditions that date back to the Apostles themselves:

- **Prayer:** "They devoted themselves to the teaching of the apostles and to the communal life, to the breaking of the bread and to the prayers" (Acts 2:42).

- **Learning:** "With great power the apostles bore witness to the resurrection of the Lord Jesus, and great favor was accorded them all" (Acts 4:33).

- **Mutual Support:** "They devoted themselves to meeting together in the temple area and to breaking bread in their homes. They ate their meals with exultation and sincerity of heart" (Acts 2:46).

- **Sharing:** "The community of believers was of one heart and mind, and no one claimed that any of his possessions was his own but they had everything in common.... There was no needy person among them, for those who owned property or houses would sell them, bring the proceeds of the sale, and put them at the feet of the apostles" (Acts 4:32, 34–35).

- **Mission:** This came through the Apostles from Christ Himself, in the earliest of the Gospels. "Go into the whole world and proclaim the gospel to every creature" (Mark 16:15). And we see His followers obeying the command and attracting others to join them. "And every day the Lord added to their number those who were being saved" (Act 2:47).

These five elements show us a pattern for Christian life. Just as they served as the pattern for the early Christians who followed after the Apostles, they likewise were the pattern for early groups of monastics as they gathered together for common prayer. These points eventually became formalized into various monastic "rules of life."

The first of these great rules was developed by St. Benedict of Nursia in the early sixth century. Benedict's first rule was to pray. In fact, the motto of Benedictines to this day is *"ora et labora"* — "prayer and work."

Benedict, now called "the Father of Western Monasticism," was under the age of 20 when he left Rome, which he viewed as decadent in lifestyle, and headed north to become a hermit. He lived in the Italian region of Subacio on a mountain ridge. But, as had happened to the Stylites and ascetics of the Middle East, Benedict soon attracted followers. He eventually founded twelve monasteries in the region around Subacio. Years later, due to persecutions, Benedict moved to Monte Cassino, where he founded the famous monastery that has lasted to this day. (Much of Monte Cassino was destroyed by Allied bombs in 1944, but it was rebuilt and rededicated in 1964.)

Monte Cassino, located even then in a highly trafficked area of Italy, soon drew the attention of pilgrims. Far from turning them away, the followers of Benedict's rule of life at Monte Cassino became, quoting Benedict's biographer, St. Gregory the Great, "the protector of the poor, their trustee, their refuge in sickness, in trial, in accidents, in want." [11]

This soon became true of monasteries all across Europe, and it changed Europe. Benedict's rule had been meant to be followed only by members of religious communities. However, since lay people soon built towns around the monasteries and chose to live in close interaction with the monks (and sisters), monastic rules for communal life soon became the rules of village life in many ways. Monasteries became the center of medieval towns, where monks took in travelers and cared for the poor and the sick. Eventually, religious orders founded hospitals, schools, universities, hospices, orphanages around the world, offering refuge to all who came their way. In these ways — through many efforts that were heroic in their own right, such as caring for plague victims — monastics spread the Gospel message.

Pope Benedict XVI called his papal namesake, and those who followed Benedict's rule of life, heralds of spiritual life that changed the life of Europe after the Roman Empire fell, and inspired "a new spiritual and cultural unity, that of the Christian faith shared by the peoples of the Continent. This is how the reality we call 'Europe' came into being." [12]

Over forty years earlier, on October 24, 1964, Pope Paul VI had said much the same when he declared Benedict the "Patron of all Europe":

(Benedict) and his sons brought, with the cross, with the book and the plow, Christian progress to the scattered populations from the Mediterranean to Scandinavia, from Ireland to the plains of Poland. With the cross — that is the law of Christ — he gave consistency to the laws and development of public and private life. To this end ... he cemented that spiritual unity in Europe under which people, divided on a linguistic, ethnic, and cultural (level), became the one people of God ... thanks to the constant efforts of (Benedict's) monks ... (that) became the hallmark of the Middle Ages. [13]

Other monastic saints followed this same pattern and changed the world around them — from St. Columbanus and the Celtic monastics in Ireland, to St. Francis and St. Anthony of Padua and their Franciscans in Italy and beyond, to the Norbertines of Belgium, and the Dominicans, the Trappists, and countless others. All sought, in their own way, what the Desert Fathers and Mothers had sought: God. That meant they followed the Holy Spirit wherever He led — into the middle of a medieval city, into foreign mission lands, or, today, into the emptiness of an increasingly secular world. They continue the work of *Santo subito*, Sainthood now.

As St. Benedict decreed in the prologue to his rule:

As we advance in the religious life and faith, we shall run the way of God's commandments with expanded hearts and unspeakable sweetness of love; so that never departing from His guidance and persevering in the monastery in His doctrine till death, we may by patience share in the sufferings of Christ, and be found worthy to be coheirs with Him of His kingdom. [14]

Perhaps advancing in the religious life, as St. Benedict advised, would even expand one's heart to such a degree that the presence of God could be found even in the fading desert daylight of a flat tire experience.

Discussion/Reflection:

1. What, if anything, appeals to you about an ascetic way of life?

2. Look at the five elements of Christian communities. Think of a group — family, parish, friends, work group — that you belong to and see how well your group measures up in these five areas. Which one do you really excel at? Which on needs more work?

3. Think about a rule of life. Look at St. Benedict's Rule. Can you write up a rule of life for yourself? For your family? Keep it simple, but be sure to put in things that will challenge you to move closer to Christ. (No poles necessary!)

CHAPTER FOUR

"There's a Man Buried under the Altar!"

Relics of Saints

In the cathedral of my home diocese, there had been a legend for many years that a body was buried under the altar. It was whispered on and speculated about, with people telling each other: "My grandmother remembers seeing it during Lent when she was little."

Now remember a few things. First, it's not odd for someone to be buried in a cathedral — many cathedrals have crypts holding the remains of their bishops and cardinals. While our own cathedral, St. Francis Xavier, does not have a crypt, it does hold the grave of the diocese's second bishop — Francis Xavier Krautbauer, who supervised the cathedral's construction — buried in the floor near the old site of the confessionals. (The story goes that Bishop Krautbauer asked to be buried there so that those coming from the confessional would walk over his grave and, perhaps, remember him in prayer.)

Secondly, most cathedrals do have parts of people buried in their altars — the relics of saints, most often pieces of bone. Our cathedral has an entire collection of relics, nearly 200. There are at least five or six first-class relics (as in bones or pieces of bone) that rest in reliquaries near the statues representing these particular saints: Agnes, Francis Xavier (the cathedral's patron), Frances Cabrini, Thérèse of Lisieux, and Anthony of Padua.

There is even one purported to be of St. Jude Thaddeus, one of the Twelve. Most of the other relics are pieces of cloth (third-class relics) and rest in the museum downstairs.

As noted earlier, the first churches erected after the early Christian house churches, were built near or directly over the graves of martyrs. Early Christians chose to be buried near either the remains of martyrs or their actual burial sites. This trend can be seen vividly in the Roman catacombs (dating back to the second century), such as the Catacomb of St. Callistus, which contains the remains of at least 50 martyrs, including St. Cecilia, the second-century virgin-martyr.

The Catholic Encyclopedia notes that this preference for being buried near martyrs had both a religious and a personal motive: "It seems to have been felt that when the souls of the blessed martyrs, on the day of general (resurrection), were once more united to their bodies, they would be accompanied in their passage to heaven by those who lay around them and that these last might, on their account, find more ready acceptance with God." [15] In other words, physical proximity to a martyr's body might help your own body gain heavenly proximity with them for eternity.

The link between churches and the physical remains of saints and martyrs continued to grow through the centuries. By 787, the Second Council of Nicaea decreed that all new churches were required to be built with relics of saints placed inside their altars. The council even said that any bishop who did not do so should be deposed. [16]

This law continued for over 1,000 years, until April 6, 1969, and the institution of the second edition of the *Roman Missal* following the Second Vatican Council. While no longer required, the custom of placing relics of saints in new altars of churches is still considered desirable, and the current *General Instruction of the Roman Missal* (2003) of the U.S. Catholic bishops notes that "The practice of the deposition of relics of saints, even those not Martyrs, under the altar to be dedicated is fittingly retained. However, care should be taken to ensure the authenticity of such relics." [17]

Trying to explain this desire to have relics of saints in our places of worship was tackled by St. Thomas Aquinas back in the thirteenth century.

> Now it is manifest that we should show honor to the saints of God, as being members of Christ, the children and friends of God, and our intercessors. Wherefore in memory of them, we ought to honor any relics of theirs in a fitting manner: principally their bodies, which were temples, and organs of the Holy Spirit dwelling and operating in them, and are destined to be likened to the body of Christ by the glory of the Resurrection. [18]

Given all this history, along with the natural desire to honor Christ through his saints and the hope to be near the holy ones in eternity, it really should be no surprise to find people believing that at least some parts of bodies were buried under our cathedral's altar. But could there be a full body underneath it?

Well, during a remodeling of the cathedral in 2004, the mystery was solved. Beneath one of the side altars, there was found a statue of the Christ in the Tomb, a life-size representation of the dead Christ lying on a slab. The side altar is crafted in such a way that oval stone windows look in at the statue, which are now open and lighted from Good Friday to Holy Saturday. At all other times, the windows are blocked over and the statue is hidden. It seems that, for many years, the windows remained blocked all year and the hidden statue behind them was forgotten — except by those spreading the legend of a body.

Christians are not alone in honoring the relics of holy people. The Israelites coming out of slavery in Egypt carried with them the bones of the patriarch Joseph, to be buried when they reached the Promised Land (see Exodus 13:19 and Joshua 24:32). The Old Testament also tells us about how the bones of the prophet Elisha raised to life a dead man who was buried in the holy man's grave (see 2 Kings 13:20–21).

Buddhists also honor their saints and preserve their cremated remains in rounded monuments called *stupas*. There were originally eight *stupas* containing the cremated remains of the Gautama Buddha (Siddhārtha Gautama), who lived about 600 years before Christ. Since then, other *stupas*, containing relics from his life or the lives of his disciples, as well as small amounts of remains from older *stupas,* have been established. For example, a *stupa* at the Mahabohdi Temple in Bihar State in India marks the site of the bohdi tree (fig tree) under which the Buddha is said to have received enlightenment. The tree itself still grows there and is much revered, as are the many trees that have been grown from it, such as a bohdi tree located at the Foster Botanical Gardens in Honolulu.

Muslims also honor relics. For them, the most holy site in the world is at Mecca in Saudi Arabia. Here can be found the Black Stone, the cornerstone of the Kaaba in the Grand Mosque. Islamic tradition says that the Black Stone (*Hajar al Aswad*) dates back to Adam and Eve and was placed in Mecca by the Prophet Mohammed. Other sacred Muslim relics might surprise many Christians because they include the sword of David, the staff of Moses, and the hand of John the Baptist — who is honored as a prophet by both Christians and Muslims. All of these relics are located in Istanbul, in the Topkapi Palace.

We must not think that the veneration of Christian relics dates only to the first martyrs of the church. The Bible itself tells us that some relics date back to the Apostles themselves. We have already noted how people were healed by the shadow of St. Peter (see Acts 5:15). But even cloths that had touched St.

Paul were considered sacred. "So extraordinary were the mighty deeds God accomplished at the hands of Paul, that when face cloths or aprons that touched his skin were applied to the sick, their diseases left them and the evil spirits came out of them" (Acts 19:11–12). Also, there are relics that the faithful date to Christ Himself, especially those of His Passion, such as the Veil of Veronica now said to rest in St. Peter's Basilica in Rome and the Crown of Thorns, which is claimed by the cathedral of *Notre Dame de Paris.* There are also relics related to the Virgin Mary.

The precious nature of the earthly remains of saints and martyrs to early Christians can be seen from documents written at the time of the martyrdom of St. Polycarp in Smyrna (now located in Turkey) in 156. After his death at the stake, Polycarp's followers were able to retrieve his remains. They wrote about this to a church in Philomelium (also in Turkey).

> We took up his bones, which are more valuable than precious stones and finer than refined gold, and laid them in a suitable place, where the Lord will permit us to gather ourselves together, as we are able, in gladness and joy, and to celebrate the birthday of his martyrdom. [19]

Clearly, Polycarp was a superhero saint to his friends and followers. No doubt, by the time they had collected his bones from the ashes, *Santo subito* was no longer a whispered prayer, but a matter of fact to them.

As centuries passed, relics of saints grew in popularity, not only as objects of veneration, but because of miracles. Miracles were even associated with the moving of relics or of parts of relics (such as a head or a hand) — called "the translation of relics" — from one site to another. From St. Bede, we heard of the translation of the relics of England's St. Cuthbert (d. 687). When the monks of his community were forced to move his body ahead of Viking invasions of Northumberland in 875 and again in 995, the saint's body was found incorrupt both times. Even his burial vestments were intact. The body finally came to rest in Durham and, since there were many miracles connected to the remains while they were in transition, there is a feast day dedicated to "the translation of St. Cuthbert" held on September 4.

Relics of the Irish St. Patrick also have many legends associated with them. These include how an angel directed St. Columba (*Colum cille*) to distribute items from the great saint's grave some 60 years after Patrick's death, including St. Patrick's Bell which was given to the town of Armagh in Northern Ireland. (Today the bell resides in the National Museum in Dublin.)

Pilgrimages to the resting places of saints became commonplace during the Middle Ages. For example, Aachen Cathedral in Germany claims to house Mary's cloak, Christ's swaddling clothes, John the Baptist's beheading cloth, and Christ's loincloth. Following a custom begun in 1349, every seven years, these relics are taken out of their shrine and put on display during the Great Aachen Pilgrimage (*Heiligtumsfahrt*).

Sacred relics eventually became listed in three ranks or classes:

- First-class relics are the bodies, or parts of bodies, of saints, and any instruments of Christ's Passion;

- Second-class relics are objects closely connected with a saint, such as something they always wore or used, perhaps their Bible or a piece of clothing;

- Third-class relics are those that came into brief contact with a saint, or which have been touched to their graves or to a first-class or second-class relic.

Years ago, my mother attended a retreat at a local Capuchin retreat house. She returned with a relic for me — a piece of cloth cut from the habit of Fr. Solanus Casey. This member of the Friars Minor Capuchin, who died in 1957 in Detroit, was declared Venerable by Pope John Paul II in 1995. He had said his first Mass at a church in the town where I was born. The relic, which I still have, could be considered a second-class relic.

Unfortunately, other, not so reverent, traditions developed around relics. During the Middle Ages, a flourishing trade arose in the business of relic-selling. It was especially common around the sites of martyrs' tombs and pilgrimage sites. Often these "sacred bones" turned out to be animal bones and countless pilgrims were duped.

By the time of the Crusades of the eleventh and twelfth centuries, the trade in relics had turned into a wholesale scramble to possess anything that had belonged to a saint or come from a holy site. Bodies of saints were fought over and sometimes desecrated, their bones captured and scattered between various sites. Some were even stolen, as in the case of St. Nicholas of Myra. In 1087, sailors — some sources call them pirates — from Bari in Italy took the saint's relics from Myra in Turkey, which had been overtaken that year by the Turks. In their haste, the sailors left some of Nicholas' bones behind. Most of these now rest in Venice, having been collected by Crusaders passing through about a decade later. (There is still a tomb for St. Nicholas that is honored in Myra, and there is a campaign to have at least some of Nicholas' remains returned there.)

The sale of relics was (and still is) formally condemned by the Catholic Church. However, that did little to stem the tide. In fact, at the Sack of Constantinople in 1204, countless relics were stolen, even by members of the clergy who were taking part in the Fourth Crusade. This drew sharp condemnation from Pope Innocent III:

> Not satisfied with breaking open the imperial treasury and plundering the goods of princes and lesser men, they also laid their hands on the treasures of the churches and,

what is more serious, on their very possessions. They have even ripped silver plates from the altars and have hacked them to pieces among themselves. They violated the holy places and have carried off crosses and relics. [20]

Relics became more and more prized and seemed to multiply, becoming another example of the excesses against which Protestant reformers railed. For example, All Saints' Church in Wittenberg Germany, called Castle Church at the time Martin Luther nailed his 95 Theses to its doors in 1517, contained more than 17,000 relics. Filling the aisles of the church, they had all been collected by Frederick III of Saxony, who was the pope's candidate for Holy Roman Emperor. (That title went to Charles V in 1519.)

The sale of relics, one aspect of the sin of simony, was never condoned by the Church. However, private individuals and even members of the clergy did sell relics and this fueled the wrath of Protestant reformers (as well as those who were seeking reforms within the Church itself). This, along with the sale of indulgences (never allowed by the Church, but sadly practiced by some local clergy) for the purpose of gaining forgiveness for sins, were two of the main religious charges against the Church that led to the Protestant Reformation.

Of course, the Catholic Church agreed with reformers on the matter of simony. In fact, it had condemned simony many times, including at the Council of Rome in 1074 and again in 1179 during the Third Lateran Council. It did so once again at the Council of Trent (1545–1563). Today, canon law (canon 1190) still expressly forbids the sale of relics. In fact, Church law even forbids the permanent transfer of relics without express permission of the Apostolic See.

Therefore, today there are only a few ways in which relics may be legitimately obtained:

- from the religious order of the saint or blessed — such as the Capuchins for Fr. Solanus;
- from a shrine of the saint;
- from the saint's home diocese;
- or from Rome itself.

For example, after the death of Pope John Paul II, the Vicariate of Rome (one of the two subdivisions of the Diocese of Rome) was freely distributing relics, made from cassocks of the late pope, to anyone who requested them.

Another charge made by Protestant reformers and connected to the saints and their relics was idolatry. The Catholic Church strongly objected to Protestant accusations of idolatry with regards to the saints, and the Council of Trent (1563) defended the practices of invoking the aid of saints through prayers and by venerating their relics and burial places. The Council fathers decreed that, since the bodies of saints had been temples of the Spirit and members of Christ's Body that were destined to be raised by Him, their relics should be "venerated by the faithful. Through them, many benefits are granted to men by God." [21]

Among the benefits of asking saints for their assistance has been the working of miracles. St. Thomas Aquinas said of such healings that even God was choosing to honor his saints. "God Himself fittingly honors such relics by working miracles at their presence." [22]

In December of 2002, Pope John Paul II approved the miracle that led to Mother Teresa of Calcutta's beatification. It involved a relic — something as simple as a medal that Mother Teresa had touched and which held her picture. By the first anniversary of Mother Teresa's death, September 5, 1998, an Indian woman named Monica Besra, mother of five, had been suffering from a large abdominal tumor for five years. Her family brought her to a hospice run by the Missionaries of Charity, who tied the medallion/locket to her stomach. The subsequent cure was deemed a miracle by the Vatican. Mother Teresa's tomb in Calcutta now draws countless visitors daily, except on Thursdays, a day of prayer in the motherhouse where she lived and where her community still ministers.

Mother Teresa is not buried under an altar. And no saint's body is buried under the altar of St. Francis Xavier Cathedral in Green Bay. However, many saints are buried under altars, including the most famous altar of the Catholic Church — the high altar of St. Peter's Basilica.

Tradition has always held that St. Peter's was built over the grave of the Chief Apostle and first pope, who was crucified in Rome during the reign of the Emperor Nero (54–68). However, not until December 1950 did a pope, Pope Pius XII, announce to the world that the tomb of Peter had definitively been found. Jesuit archaeologists had been working for ten years under the Vatican basilica and were certain that the tomb was that of Peter. Even then, however, the bones within could not be positively identified.

Work continued and, on June 26, 1968, another pope, Pope Paul VI, was able to announce that the bones under the basilica were indeed those of St. Peter. Those bones had been scientifically identified as those of a man in his sixties, the reported age of Peter when he died in A.D. 67. The tomb itself lies directly below the main altar in St. Peter's, two stories down and beneath the Vatican grottoes.

There's another man beneath another altar in Rome. In 2006, Vatican archaeologist Giorgio Filippi declared that his team had unearthed the stone coffin believed to be that of St. Paul (also martyred during the reign of Nero) from under the altar of the Basilica of St. Paul Outside-the-Walls, just outside the old city of Rome. The sarcophagus holding the remains had lain about five feet below the papal altar. In 2009, Pope Benedict XVI announced that carbon-14 dating of remains from inside the coffin had confirmed that they were from the first century and could indeed be that of the Apostle to the Gentiles. This confirmation of Paul's resting place — right where tradition had said — was probably delayed because the basilica had been nearly destroyed by fire in 1823 and was largely rebuilt.

So there are definitely two men buried under altars — two of the greatest saints of the Church resting under altars in two of the greatest churches of the Catholic faith. Their graves continue to draw people to Rome, the heart of the Church, but they also draw us beyond Rome and to Christ through the Sacrifice, offered each day on countless altars, that is the true heart of the Catholic Church.

Discussion/Reflection:

1. What do you think about relics of saints? Do they seem a little unusual?

2. Have you ever discussed relics with someone who isn't Catholic? How would you explain relics to them?

3. Do you have a relic of a saint, like my relic of Francis Solanus Casey? How did you come by it and what does it mean to you?

4. Do you have a relic from someone in your life who has been like a saint to you? What is it? What makes it special?

CHAPTER FIVE

Enough is Enough;
You're Not a Saint Anymore

Rules for "Official" Saints

"Enough is enough, and enough is too much."

While Pope Alexander III probably had little in common with Popeye the Sailor Man, he might have related to these well-known words of the heroic spinach-eater of the comics. The occasion was the growing veneration of a locally-acclaimed saint in Sweden. It seems that the purported holy man had actually been killed, not as a martyr, but in the midst of a drunken brawl. (Some sources believe the deceased was Erik, the father of the king of that time.) Alexander III wrote to King Knut I of Sweden in 1171 or 1172 and asserted the papal prerogative to proclaim saints, largely because of this incident. "Even if miracles were worked through him," the pope wrote, "it is not lawful for you to venerate him as a saint without the authority of the Roman Church." [23] To this day, St. Erick, patron of Sweden, has not been officially canonized by the Catholic Church.

No one is really certain if Pope Alexander was asserting a newly established reservation of authority to name saints to the papal office or restating a long held tradition by which popes, or at least papal councils, ratified canonizations. For example, it wasn't until 993, when Pope John XV canonized Ulrich, bishop of Augsberg, that a pope actually canonized a saint. It was a papal first.

In a follow-up letter to the bishops of Sweden in 1173, Pope Alexander III directly ordered that no canonizations could take place without the approval of Rome. Whether he meant only in Sweden or worldwide was debated. Either way, his position was confirmed by his successor, Innocent III, shortly after. It was 1200, and the canonization that brought up the question was that of St. Cunegundes, an empress of the Holy Roman Empire. Pope Innocent III used a papal bull (official papal document stamped with a lead seal or *bulla*) to confirm Alexander III's position.

Then, in 1234, Pope Gregory IX issued a decree saying that no one could be honored as a saint by the universal Church who had not first been given that title by the Roman pontiff. That made it universal church law. Finally, in the seventeenth century, Pope Urban VII (1634) reserved to the pope the right to beatify anyone as well, thus taking most of the canonization procedure out of the hands of local bishops for all time.

But not all parts of the canonization process are the venue of Rome, especially not the groundwork for a sainthood cause.

Since the days of the early Church, as we saw with martyrs, it has been the local communities who first honored and venerated holy people as saints. These included the Apostles, martyrs and other early exemplars of the Faith. Because bishops are the heads of the local churches, it was natural that they first oversaw these honors and eventually developed the rites and procedures for honoring saints.

These customs eventually led to compiling lists of saints, known as martyrologies. These could be as simple as a listing of the saints and martyrs honored by local churches or as elaborate as complete biographies of these individuals, along with calendars of their feast days and specific liturgical ceremonies for those feast days. *The Catholic Encyclopedia* notes that the earliest of these martyrologies may date to the fifth century, although the first official one was called the *Hieronymian*. (The *Hieronymian* has been incorrectly attributed to St. Jerome — who died in 420 — because his full name in Latin was Eusebius Sophronius *Hieronymus*.) The earliest martyrologies seem to have come to the universal Church through the Eastern Catholic churches as well as the churches of northern Africa. One famous martyrology is attributed to the work of St. Bede in the eighth century.

However, the most famous of all may have been the legend-rich book of saints known as *The Golden Legend*. This medieval best-seller was compiled in 1260 by Blessed Jacobus de Voragine, a Dominican priest and archbishop of Genoa. It contained legends of various saints and even legends related to relics of saints. From here we get stories of saints and talking animals and wondrous miracles. After the printing press was invented in 1450, *The Golden Legend* became the most popular book in Europe between 1470 and 1530; it had more editions than the Bible at the time and was printed in every major European language. However, its accuracy came into question in later centuries and it eventually fell from notice.

What's interesting about the early martyrologies is that local churches set their own feast days for saints. Called *feria* — for the Latin word for "free day" — these days became local holidays. Even slaves received the day off. Local fairs sprang up, with entertainers and peddlers traveling from town to town, following the feasts. (And, as we have seen, the same was true for "relic sellers.") By the Middle Ages, most regions had at least thirty, even as many as sixty, annual feast days for local saints. Since these holidays were marked in addition to the universal Church's official feasts, such as Christmas and Easter, as well as Sundays, that meant there were a lot of days off from work!

Because it meant increased income for the local economy from pilgrims, peddlers, and visiting dignitaries, it became a matter of competition — just as it had been with relics — to have a local saint with his or her own feast day located right in your town. Pilgrims would come from great distances to venerate the tomb of the saint for his or her feast day, bringing a regular source of income for towns and their surrounding regions. For the better known saints, this could lead to major road and transportation development. (Remember the trains and St. Jean-Marie Vianney?)

- For example, the feast day of St. James, July 25, is a huge celebration in Santiago de Compostella, Spain, where the relics of this apostle have been venerated since at least the eighth century.

- In England, the tomb of St. Hugh put the town of Lincoln on the map as a great pilgrimage site from the thirteenth century until the time of Henry VIII. (Chaucer's *Canterbury Tales* — another hit of the fourteenth century — and its mention of the saintly "Little Hugh" helped as well.)

- And Saint-Maximin-la-Sainte-Baume in Toulouse, France, became famous in the twelfth century as the site of the tomb of Mary Magdalene. A huge cathedral built there drew pilgrims, even during its construction, which took the next three centuries.

However, with so many feast days, relics, and local saints, matters became increasingly difficult to authenticate. We've already seen this problem with relics and, given the link between relics and pilgrimage sites, matters simmered. Even in the fourth century, St. Augustine of Hippo was denouncing the sale of false relics by clerical imposters who travelled from region to region, preying on the gullible. This included the use of false relics to establish holy sites to attract pilgrims. Finally, in 1215, the Fourth Lateran Council forbade the sale of relics and restricted the authentication of any new relics to the pope. "In the future," the council added, "prelates shall not permit those who come to their churches *causa venerationis* to be deceived by worthless fabrications or false documents as has been done in many places for the sake of gain" (canon 62). [24]

Still, matters (and fairs, pilgrimages, and celebrations) continued much the same, despite the stricter rules. And they fueled the wrath of reformers of all sorts, including the Protestants in the sixteenth century. In 1543, John Calvin condemned the prevalence of false relics in the Catholic Church, citing the myriad examples of relics of the Cross of Christ.

"Now let us consider how many relics of the true cross there are in the world," Calvin wrote. "An account of those merely with which I am acquainted would fill a whole volume.... Large splinters of it are preserved in various places, as for instance in the Holy Chapel at Paris, whilst at Rome they show a crucifix of considerable size made entirely, they say, from this wood. In short, if we were to collect all these pieces of the true cross exhibited in various parts, they would form a whole ship's cargo." [25]

Even today, the proliferation of false relics continues. A recent search of eBay revealed 3,128 "Christian relics" for sale, including 13 purported to be of the True Cross for bids ranging from $315 to $3,990. (There were also relics from other religious traditions, including Buddhist relics.)

Of course, the Catholic Church has always tried to deal with these problems. Even St. Helen herself, after discovering the True Cross in Jerusalem in 327, had to deal with authenticating her find. She lacked the scientific methods we would employ in the twenty-first century, but she did her best with what she had. According to legend, when Helen found three crosses buried near Jerusalem's old city walls, she was left with the dilemma of how to determine which one, if any, was Christ's. So she touched each cross to a sick woman in her retinue. When the woman was healed instantly by one of the crosses, her healing was accepted as a sign of the relic's authenticity. Helen, with the authority of her son, the Emperor Constantine, had a church built to house the Cross in Jerusalem. This was the beginning of what became the Church of the Holy Sepulchre, the destination of many pilgrims to this day.

Of course, authentication has improved over the centuries. Today, relics from saints are authenticated by various tests, including carbon dating. Yet, even these methods do not settle the point at all times. Carbon-14 tests in 1988 dated the Shroud of Turin, believed by many to be the burial cloth of Jesus Christ and housed at the cathedral in Turin since 1578, to the Middle Ages, or about 600 years ago, thus disqualifying it as a first-century relic. However, in late 2011, Italy's national research agency (National Agency for New Technologies, Energy, and Sustainable Economic Development, or ENEA) reported a study that questioned the "fifteenth-century fake" claim. ENEA said that it had tried to replicate yellow markings that appear on the Shroud and was only able to do so after five years of work, using ultra-violet lasers. ENEA therefore concluded that a relic of this complexity would have been beyond the technology of medieval times. Finally, in 2013, when the Shroud was put on public display for Holy Saturday, results of a new study by the University of Padua, using the same fibers tested in 1988, dated the fabric to the time of Christ, saying that the 1988 test had been flawed by using repair fibers rather than original material.

The search for the truth about the Shroud continues and acceptance of it as Jesus' burial cloth remains as it always has, a matter of personal belief. Small wonder, then, that the Vatican chooses to restrict declaration of saints — and their relics and feast days — to itself.

The Calendar of Saints — the Church's official list of the feast days of saints — tries to put some order to the vast array of holy people honored the world over. The first Roman Martyrology dates to the fifth century. The first edition of the current "Roman Martyology" appeared in 1583 under Pope Gregory XIII; a revised edition appeared the next year and was approved for use in the universal church.

Still, local calendars of feast days are still allowed and their approval is left to local bishops. For the universal Church, however, the official martyrology controls the calendar. The Second Vatican Council, recognizing that there were changes needed, decreed that, in any new martyrology — the last edition prior to Vatican II was in 1956 — "the accounts of martyrdom or the lives of the saints are to accord with the facts of history." (Translation: "Most legends didn't count.") Due to the proliferation of the number of feast days over the centuries, the Council in its Constitution on the Sacred Liturgy proposed, "Lest the feasts of the saints should take precedence over the feasts which commemorate the very mysteries of salvation, many of them should be left to be celebrated by a particular Church, or nation, or family of religious. Only those should be extended to the universal Church which commemorate saints who are truly of universal importance" (*Sacrosanctum Concilium*, No. 111).

In effect, this meant that many saints were suddenly off the official celebration list. Following upon this, in 1969, Pope Paul VI issued an apostolic letter, *Mysterii Paschalis*. The most notable effect of this letter was to suppress the celebration of feast days of any saints whose history was regarded as more legend than fact.

This was when St. Christopher "became no longer a saint," as some dismayed travelers mistakenly assume. Christopher — the patron of travelers who is said to have carried the Christ Child on his shoulders — is still a saint. However, his feast day — July 25 — is no longer on the official calendar of the universal Church. This does not mean that Christopher cannot be honored on that day by local churches, such as in Anatolia in Asia Minor, where it is said that he died in the third century. And, yes, travelers and drivers can still have St. Christopher medals in their vehicles and use them to pray for safe journeys.

Another interesting case is that of St. Catherine of Alexandria, whose martyrdom in Egypt in A.D. 305 on a large wheel has been remembered every Fourth of July with a firework known as St. Catherine's Wheel. (This pyrotechnic display is especially popular on the island of Malta.) St. Catherine was also removed from the official church calendar in 1970, along with St. Christopher. However, in 2002, Pope John Paul II used his own authority and reinstated her feast day (Nov. 25), putting it back on the calendar of the universal Church. (No doubt many fireworks on Malta marked the event.)

The Roman Martyrology released in 2004 was an 844-page volume that listed the names of 6,500 people who have been beatified and/or canonized. Its list continues to be updated as new saints are added, including the 482 added during Pope John Paul II's pontificate. That was a record in his day, but it was short-lived. Pope Francis, on May 12, 2013, canonized 802 saints, and that's a hefty number, even for someone of Popeye's strength.

Discussion/Reflection:

1. Who is the most unusual saint you've heard about?

2. Do you have a St. Christopher medal, or remember seeing a statue of him in someone's car? Imagine if a favorite saint of yours was "demoted" and removed from the calendar. How would you feel?

3. What are your thoughts about the Shroud of Turin, or other relics of Christ such as fragments of the True Cross? How are such relics helpful to faith life?

Just Four Easy (Sort of) Steps

The Canonization Process

When I was little, I found this really old book — at least it was one volume of a set of really old books. I dragged it everywhere, in the way that many other kids would drag around comic books, Mother Goose stories, a Hardy Boys mystery, or a bag of marbles. (Today, I would have it all on a computer tablet.) I remember reading the book in the car, sitting in the beauty salon while Mom got her hair done, and even climbing up in the elm tree in the front yard with it. The book was old and tattered, and full of stories about saints — and how they traveled as missionaries, preached, and taught, and how many of them died as martyrs — sometimes in vivid detail. I really liked people like St. Lawrence, who was grilled to death, but asked his executioners to "turn me over because I'm done on this side." The man was dying and still making jokes! He must have been a fun person to be around.

It turns out that I had a copy of part of Blessed Jacobus' *Butler's Lives of the Saints*, first published between 1756 and 1759. (I probably had a copy of the 1956 edition.) The original edition listed about 1,500 saints; the 1956 edition had 2,565. I never counted the ones in my book, but I reread many of the stories. Over and over.

If I had found a copy of *The Golden Legend*, I might never have put it down. This medieval best-seller has had a bit of a revival, thanks to the Internet, but will probably never reach its fifteenth and sixteenth century fame again.

During the same time that *The Golden Legend* rose to prominence and then faded from popularity, the process of recognizing a saint — canonization — was also being formalized. However, just as it has been since the early days of *Santo subito*, the process still really started in about that same way — with a story. Or with many stories.

Today, the process for canonization begins at the diocesan level, in the diocese where the proposed saint died. (Sometimes, a cause is opened in the diocese where the person worked, as was the case for John Paul II.) A waiting period of five years after the proposed saint's death must be observed, but can be waived by the pope. This happened in the causes of both Mother Teresa and Pope John Paul II. (In the case of John Paul II, this led to a modern record, with his canonization taking place less than nine years after his death. The modern record prior to that had been St. Josemaría Escrivá, who died on June 26, 1975, and was canonized by Pope John Paul II on October 6, 2002.)

The basic purpose of this waiting period is to allow for the initial fervor following a holy person's death to settle and for what is called "a cult" (from the Latin *cultus*, meaning "to venerate") honoring the person to germinate. It means that diocesan officials can wait to see if the cries of "*Santo subito*" die down, or get louder. Remember what Gamaliel told the Sanhedrin about leaving things alone to see if they come from God or not (see Acts 5:35–39)? The waiting period for saints follows the same idea.

Servant of God

After the waiting period, the local bishop is allowed to petition Rome for permission to begin the sainthood cause. He can do this on his own or after a formal request is presented to him, often by a religious community to which the proposed saint belonged. So, just as in the earliest days, the local bishop still has first authority in a sainthood cause. Pope John Paul II set this into law in January 1983 when he said that all bishops had the rights, either on their own or at the request of the faithful, to start the inquiry into the lives of martyrs and other holy people. He also said that bishops have the responsibility to study any reported miracles and otherwise "inquire about the life, virtues, or martyrdom and reputation of sanctity or martyrdom, alleged miracles ... related to the Servant of God, whose canonization is sought." [26]

If Rome does not object, a bishop opens a sainthood cause and the person may then be called "Servant of God" (*Servus Dei*). There's a custom that when the bishop announces the opening of a sainthood cause, he hangs an official notice to that effect on the door of the cathedral. This edict also serves to notify the faithful that they may present testimony about the life of the proposed saint to include in the study of the cause. At this point, a postulator (from a Latin verb meaning "to ask," or even "to demand") is appointed. Locally, this person — either a priest or a lay person — must be expert in theological, canonical, and historical matters, as well as versed in the practice of the Congregation for the Causes of Saints.

Testimony about the Servant of God's life is sought and his or her writings, if any exist, are reviewed. If sufficient evidence of a virtuous life is found, the bishop declares that the heroic virtues of the Servant of God have been demonstrated and refers the cause to the Vatican and its sainthood congregation. All documents pertaining to the cause are sent to Rome, where it is turned over to another postulator who resides in Rome. This person will take up the case once directed to do so by the sainthood congregation. When the approved cause for canonization — the formal collection of documents for review — is sent to Rome, it is called the *positio* (*Positio super Virtutibus*). This *positio* will contain massive amounts of information about how the proposed saint lived and how he or she died. This should include a biography or at least an accurate chronology of the life and deeds of the person, including details on his/her virtues, martyrdom (if such is the case), reputation of sanctity, and any reported miracles. "Nor should anything be omitted which seems to be contrary or less favorable to the cause." [27] Sort of a "warts and all" approach. After all, we have to realize that saints were also human and had their rough edges. For example, any *positio* today about the great St. Jerome would need to include that he had a temper.

When the *positio* of Archbishop Fulton Sheen was present-ed in Rome on May 25, 2011, it contained nearly 2,000 pages of material. The noted media personality had written 73 books in his lifetime and appeared on radio (beginning in 1930 and lasting un-til his television appearances began) and on television from 1951–57 and again from 1961–68. When he had to, the archbishop used his Irish sense of humor and is credited with saying: "Hearing nuns' confessions is like being stoned to death with popcorn."

As Bishop Daniel Jenky of Peoria, Illinois, said when he presented the *positio*, "I don't know how many people he brought to the faith; it must be thousands and thousands. He never passed by an opportunity to bring someone to the faith. He was a hands-on evangelizer." [28]

Venerable

The Vatican began its review of the Peoria material. Thirteen months later, on June 28, 2012, Pope Benedict XVI approved the heroic virtues of Fulton J. Sheen. At this point, for Arch-bishop Fulton Sheen, or for any person proposed for sainthood, the investigation stage had reached a point that showed he had led a life of heroic proportion, worthy of imitation. A "Decree of Heroic Virtues" was prepared and sent to the Holy Father for approval. When this approval is received, it brings the official title of "Venerable" to the proposed saint.

During those thirteen months for Archbishop Sheen's cause, the Congregation for the Causes of Saints was reading the story of Fulton Sheen. Experts, called "relators," in fields like history or communications or theology, pored over those 2,000 pages and gave their opinion about the virtues of the life of Fulton Sheen. If Archbishop Sheen had died as a martyr, the congregation would also have reviewed the stories of witnesses to the circumstances surrounding his death. Such was the case for Maximilian Kolbe, the Franciscan saint who died in the Nazi death camp at Auschwitz on Aug. 14, 1941, after offering himself in place of another condemned man. Among those stories heard by the relators in the cause of Father Kolbe was that of Bruno Borowiec, a Polish man who had been assigned as a janitorial assistant in the Auschwitz starvation bunker. Before Borowiec died in 1947, he told his story to his own parish priest:

> "The ten condemned to death went through terrible days. From the underground cell in which they were shut up there continually arose the echo of prayers and canticles.... Father Kolbe never asked for anything and did not complain, rather he encouraged the others, saying that the fugitive might be found and then they would all be freed. One of the SS guards remarked: 'This priest is really a great man. We have never seen anyone like him.'
>
> "Two weeks passed in this way. Meanwhile one after another they died, until only Father Kolbe was left. This, the authorities felt, was too long. The cell was needed for new victims. So one day they brought in the head of the sick-quarters, a German named Bock, who gave Father Kolbe an injection of carbolic acid in the vein of his left

arm. Father Kolbe, with a prayer on his lips, himself gave his arm to the executioner. Unable to watch this, I left under the pretext of work to be done. Immediately after the SS men had left, I returned to the cell, where I found Father Kolbe leaning in a sitting position against the back wall with his eyes open and his head drooping sideways. His face was calm and radiant." [29]

There could be no doubt about the heroic virtues of this priest, and Father Kolbe was beatified in 1971 and canonized on October 10, 1982. Present in Vatican Square on that October day was Franciszek Gajowniczek, the man whose life was spared when Father Kolbe took his place.

Beatified — Raised to the Altar

"How blessed are the feet of those who bring good news."

While a miracle must be approved after the death of a proposed saint before they can be beatified — to show that this person is at this moment in the presence of God and is able to intercede for those of us still on earth — this is not the case with a martyr such as Maximilian Kolbe. Once martyrdom has been ascertained by the sainthood congregation, a Servant of God may immediately be beatified at the approval of the pope. No reported and subsequently approved miracles are needed because their death is considered to be a miracle of grace.

For the rest of those on the path to sainthood, however, proof of a miracle is required before beatification may take place. While a broad range of miracles have been attributed to the intervention of saints from early days — from the third-century St. Denis, who was beheaded but is also said to have picked up his head and preached a sermon afterwards, to the twelfth-century St. Isidore the Farmer, whose angel plowed his fields while Isidore prayed or attended Mass — at this point in history, we most often look for miracles in medically documented cures that can be attributed to the intercession of one of the venerable.

We have all experienced what we might call miracles — from the birth of children to the fact that we make it through a tough work week with our jobs intact. However, for the Vatican, a miracle has to be scrutinized by experts in fields ranging from theology to science and medicine.

To be approved, a miracle must meet four requirements:

- It must be immediate;
- It must be complete;
- It must be permanent;
- And it must be unexplainable by scientific means.

Again, the role of local bishops is crucial. The miracle to be considered is either presented in the diocese in which it occurred or in which the Venerable died. The bishop there must then have the miracle examined by both scientific and theological experts. If the miracle passes the local tribunal's scrutiny, the bishop must then decide whether to present the miracle to the Vatican. There, the entire process of scrutiny is repeated under the direction of the Vatican's Congregation of Sainthood Causes. The Congregation maintains its own medical commission, an international board of experts that reviews all unexplained medical miracles presented for beatification or canonization causes. This group's anonymity is strictly maintained. It was this board that approved the medical cure that moved the beatification cause of Pope John Paul II forward.

"All I can tell you is that I was sick and now I am cured. It is for the church to say and to recognize whether it is a miracle," Sr. Marie Simon Pierre, a French member of the Little Sisters of Catholic Motherhood, told various news outlets in 2007, claiming that the intercession of the late pontiff had led to her cure of

Parkinson's Disease. While her renewed health was enough for Sister Marie Simon to believe in John Paul's sainthood, it was not enough for the Vatican to decide to proclaim it as a miracle from God. Instead, an investigation was started, following the guidelines above. According to Catholic News Service, the postulator of Pope John Paul's cause, Msgr. Slawomir Oder, said that these investigations included testimony from theologians and canon lawyers, physicians, a psychiatrist, and a handwriting expert, since a patient's handwriting can serve as an indicator of the progress of Parkinson's disease. (A condition called micrographia, an increasingly smaller size and more cramped style in making letters, is a symptom of Parkinson's.) Sister Marie Simon's handwriting was checked. Only after all this work was completed, and even more that we don't know about, did the Vatican certify this cure as an authentic miracle on January 14, 2011. This opened the door for John Paul's beatification, which took place on May 1, 2011.[30] (On September 30, 2013, the Vatican announced the date for his canonization: April 27, 2014.)

When a person is beatified, they are technically "raised to the altar." This means that, in certain regions or among certain religiously affiliated groups, a memorial Mass may be celebrated on a certain feast day in honor of the Blessed. However, for the universal Church to be able to celebrate the feast day of a holy one, formal canonization must have taken place. It should also be noted that, at this stage in the canonization process, the beatification is not considered to be an infallible act, as is the case with canonization. The act of formal canonization is believed to be protected from error by the actions of the Holy Spirit.

Canonized — Raised to the Altars of the Saints

A second miracle, one that is verified as taking place after be-atification, is needed for a declaration of sainthood. Unless, of course, the pope decides otherwise.

Such was the case on July 5, 2013, when Pope Francis announced that Blessed John XXIII — known the world over as "the Good Pope" (*Il Papa buono* in Italian) — would be canonized without the requisite second miracle. As Vatican spokesman Father Federico Lombardi, S.J., explained it to the media, even though there had been no second miracle approved, it was the Pope's desire and decision that the sainthood of "the Pope of the Second Vatican Council" be recognized. [31] It also proved to be a prime example of a "*Santo subito*" declaration, voiced by a pope himself.

The exception proves the rule, however, since the usual process for canonization follows the same pattern as for beatification and starts with the local bishop. Once a second miracle is verified, the Blessed (the *Beatus*) is formally recognized by the pope as a saint of the universal church and his or her feast day is approved for celebration worldwide ("raised to the altars," the universal altars instead of only the local regional altar that honors a Blessed).

The term "canonization" comes from the word "*canon*" which, in the Church, often refers to laws — as in "canon law." However, "the Canon of Saints" means something a little different than rules. Instead, it's more like a term of measurement.

The Greek word *kanon* means "straight" and is similar to the Hebrew word *kaneh* which refers to reeds, which are also straight. The Canon of Saints is a roll call of those holy people whose paths, the church believes, led them straight to God. By following their examples, we can be assured of a straight path as well.

The bishops of the Second Vatican Council told us that when we honor the saints, especially on their feast days, "the Church proclaims the Paschal Mystery achieved in the saints who have suffered and been glorified with Christ; she proposes them to the faithful as examples drawing all to the Father through Christ and, through their merits, she pleads for God's favors" (*Sacrosanctum Concilium*, No. 104).

One final thing to remember is that, while the pope approves sainthood causes, the Holy Father does not "make someone a saint." That's God's turf. All formal canonization does is state that the Church believes that the holy person who has been raised to the altars is present with God at this very moment and can both intercede for us and provide us with an example to follow on how to live a holy life. It's the Church's way of saying "Yes" to the cry of "*Santo subito.*" "Sainthood now" is confirmed.

Discussion/Reflection:

1. Who is a recent saint whom you remember being canonized? Is there a "Venerable" or a "Blessed" whom you hope will soon be canonized? Why are they important to you?

2. What's a miracle by your own definition? Have you witnessed a miracle?

3. Which saint do you most often ask for help? Why?

4. If you were ever to be "raised to the altars," what would you most like to help people with from heaven?

CHAPTER SEVEN

Three Birthdays

Feast Days of Saints

Three candles on three cakes.

Birthday cakes are wonderful. When I was little, there were always candles on the cake: one candle for each year.

However, after a while, I began to notice that adults in the family only had three candles on their cakes. I always supposed that was because there wasn't enough room on their cakes for all the candles that they needed.

"No," my Nana explained, "the three candles are for the past, the present, and the future." And that, she felt, covered everything anyone needed.

When we celebrate the feast days of canonized saints, it is not their birthdays that we celebrate. For example, the feast day of St. Thérèse of Lisieux, the Little Flower, is not January 2, the day she was born in 1873. Rather, it is October 1.

Why?

Because Thérèse died on September 30 (in 1897), which is close to Oct. 1. (St. Jerome, the great Bible saint, already had September 30 as his feast day.) Unlike those of us still on our earthly journey, the birthdays of saints don't matter that much. Instead, what's usually honored is the day on which they died — or as close to it as possible. The feast day of St. John Paul II is one of the exceptions: October 22, the anniversary of his 1978 installation as pope.

Marking a saint's feast day on the day when he or she died is not done as a sign of mourning, but rather as a sign of joy. The days on which saints died are remembered as their true *dies natalis*, their "birthdays," but their *dies natalis* in a new way: their birthdays into heaven — celebrations of their passing from this world into eternal life with God. As we explored earlier, the first saints were often martyrs and the days on which they died were celebrated as the days that marked the acts of faith and sacrifice by which they glorified God.

So an individual's birthday is not usually marked as a big event in the life of the Church. (Of course, the feast of Pentecost, sometimes called the birthday of the Church, is a truly big event. However, that's because it's a *dia natalis* for the whole Church and not just for one person.) This practice of not noting a birthday wasn't much different than what the secular world did around the time of the infant Church. For the average person in the Middle East of the first century, a birthday wasn't a big deal. In part, that was due to the high rates of infant mortality. In ancient Rome of the time, infant mortality was one in four. In fact, for developing countries to this day, life expectancy at age one jumps markedly higher than it was at birth. In other words, if a baby survives to its first birthday, it starts to look like he or she has a pretty good chance of making it to adulthood. So that first birthday was when people could really think about celebrations.

In Jewish tradition — from which the early Church grew — birthdays were not usually celebrated either. In the Bible, in fact, birthdays are rarely noted. When they are, it is not often under favorable circumstances. In the Old Testament, the only birthday directly mentioned is that of Pharaoh, not long before the Israelites became slaves in Egypt (see Genesis 40:20–22). It was on this day that Pharaoh had his chief baker executed, just as the enslaved Joseph had predicted when interpreting the poor man's dream while they shared a prison cell. At the time, it was a good day for Joseph, who became Vizier for Pharaoh, but it eventually led to his people's enslavement. Then there was Moses, whose birth earned him an immediate death sentence, as it did all Hebrew males of his day.

In the New Testament, birthdays weren't so wonderful either. The only birthday noted there is Herod Antipas' birthday — because that was when he had John the Baptist beheaded, at the request of Herodias's daughter.

The only other birthday (besides, of course, Jesus') hinted at in the Bible was related to Job's first ten children (seven sons and three daughters), who were all killed in a windstorm while they were dining together. While our Catholic translation of the Book of Job doesn't mention it as a birthday celebration, some versions of the account — such as the King James Bible — translate verse four in Chapter One as saying that the siblings often gathered together for their birthday feasts and that they died while celebrating the feast of the eldest brother.

Celebrating birthdays just weren't high points in biblical history. In fact, in most ancient societies, only the birthdays of kings were ever remembered and celebrated. This is, of course, why Jesus' birth was eventually celebrated as a feast — but not until the fourth century; this was at the time when the emperors of Rome fully embraced the Christian faith and decreed that the King of all Kings should receive royal honors. So a birthday feast — the Nativity — was in order. Around that same time, the birth of John the Baptist also rose to honor — since it was clearly indicated in Luke's Gospel as tied to the mystery of the Incarnation.

In fact, to this day, there are only three birthdays which the Church honors as feast days. And they can be thought of as our Three Candles: past, present, and future. Let's take them in chronological order.

The Past

John the Baptist is honored as the Precursor of Christ, prophet of the Most High and last of the Old Testament prophets. From Elizabeth's womb, he heralds the Gospel and rejoices in the Incarnation. He prepares for the Lamb of God with his baptism of repentance and bears witness to Christ by his own testimony and by his martyr's death.

While the Church celebrates the day of John's martyrdom — August 29, officially called the Passion of John the Baptist — just as it does all the other saints, the birthday of John is also celebrated: on June 24. This date was arbitrarily set to fall six months before Christmas because the Angel Gabriel, when he appeared to Mary at the Annunciation, told her that her kinswoman, Elizabeth — the mother of John — was "in her sixth month." Based on the date of Jesus' Nativity, formalized around the fourth century as December 25, that brings us to John's birth in June. The 24th was set by using the Roman system of dating: counting backwards (in this case, eight days) from the first day of the month following. December has 31 days and June has 30, so counting back eight days from the first of the respective month following leads to the 25th of December and the 24th of June respectively. (The eighth day was when Jesus was circumcised and that feast is celebrated on January 1. John's eighth day would have been July 1.) As we see from Matthew's Gospel (Luke 2:21), it was far more important to mark that a baby boy had been circumcised — made a son of the covenant — than to worry about his birthday. This day was also when a boy received his name. Luke tells us (in Luke 1:13) that John received the name given him by the angel who appeared to Zechariah, the priest, while he was offering sacrifice in the Temple.

John is a hinge point in Christian history — his story appears at the beginning of the New Testament and marks the culmination of the Old. As the *Catechism of the Catholic Church* tells us, "By celebrating the precursor's birth and martyrdom, the Church unites herself to his desire: 'He must increase, but I must decrease'" (CCC 524).

Just as John decreased and Jesus increased, so does the past turn to the present and looks to the future within the cycle of the Church year. This is why Advent marks the beginning of the liturgical year: it marks the hinge point of the past with the present and the future.

In ancient Rome, there was a god named Janus, who had two faces — one looking forward and one looking back. Janus was the god of gates, of beginnings and endings. The month of January, the beginning of our secular year, is named after Janus. The season of Advent — the beginning of our church year — also looks in both directions. The Roman Calendar reminds us of the double meaning of the season: "Advent has a twofold character: as a season to prepare for Christmas when Christ's first coming to us is remembered; as a season when that remembrance directs the mind and heart to await Christ's Second Coming at the end of time" [32].

John's life had that same two-fold nature and his birthday serves to remind us that our own lives draw from the past and turn to the eternal future.

The Present

In Bethlehem, we can find the Church of the Nativity. But did you know that, in Jerusalem, you can find a church honoring the birth of the Blessed Virgin?

It is the Church of St. Anne, built in A.D. 1100 over the remains of a sixth-century basilica. In a grotto beneath the church — the best preserved of Jerusalem's Crusader churches — is a site revered as the remains of the house of Anne and Joachim, Mary's parents, and the birthplace of their child, Mary.

St. Anne's Church sits very near the Temple Mount, beside the Sheep Gate and the Pool of Bethesda. This was the pool used to prepare the sacrificial animals for the Temple. It was also known for its healing qualities, even before Jesus cured a man there (John 5).

Little is really known about Mary's birth or birthplace — nothing appears in the canonical Gospels, although the apocryphal *Protoevangelium of St. James* of the late first century mentions the circumstances of the Virgin's birth. This is where we find the story of her parents and of their childless state before Mary was born to them. Early in her life, according to the *Protoevangelium*, Mary was presented at the Temple by her parents and became one of the virgins who lived and studied there during childhood. These virgins were also charged with weaving the Temple Veil that was hung before the Holy of Holies. Whether or not Mary was born in Jerusalem, there is much symbolic insight gained by linking her birthplace to the Temple area and to the Temple veil which was rent when her Son died on the Cross.

The Temple was where God chose to reside among His Chosen People. The first Temple — not the Temple of Mary's time, but the one built by King Solomon — housed the Ark of the Covenant. (The Ark disappeared after the Babylonian destruction of Jerusalem and the Temple in 587 B.C.) One of Mary's titles is "Ark of the New Covenant." This is because she is recognized as the living Temple in which Jesus, God incarnate, first came to dwell.

The celebration of a feast in honor of Mary's birth dates back to sixth century in Jerusalem. From there, it spread through the Eastern Christian churches, especially in Syria. A century later, the feast reached Rome, but it did not become a major feast there until the thirteenth century.

While generally celebrated in September, Mary's nativity has also been marked in May (placing it before John the Baptist's on the calendar). Today it is celebrated on September 8, exactly nine months after the Feast of the Immaculate Conception of Mary. (While the Immaculate Conception was not declared a dogma of the Church until 1854, it is ancient in tradition, and celebrations of Mary's birthday dating back to the sixth century in the Eastern churches were celebrated under the title of the Conception of St. Anne.)

St. Andrew of Crete, in the eighth century, explained Mary's important role, her link to the Temple, and even her Immaculate Conception, in the homily on a feast day of Mary's birth: "This is, in fact, the day on which the Creator of the world constructed His temple; today is the day on which, by a stupendous project, a creature becomes the preferred dwelling of the Creator." [33]

Beyond that, what does the feast of Mary's nativity mean for Christians today, in the modern present?

- First, as St. Andrew said, Mary was the vessel in which Christ took on human flesh, the same flesh we share with him today. Through Mary's humanity, we who are alive today become brothers and sisters of that Word made Flesh.

- Second, the Church teaches that Mary was conceived without sin. This makes her unique among all other humans. Yet, *how* was Mary preserved from sin? In the same way we are redeemed from sin to this day: through Christ.

- Mary was chosen and, like us — though in a different fashion — redeemed. The *Catechism of the Catholic Church*, quoting both St. Paul and the Fathers of Vatican II, states that "(Mary) is 'redeemed, in a more exalted fashion, by the reason of the merits of her Son.' The Father blessed Mary more than any other created person 'in Christ with every spiritual blessing'" (CCC 492).

- As this chosen one of God, Mary was the first to benefit from the salvation brought to all by Christ, even before she was born. All of us likewise benefit from that salvation. We, like Mary, are saved by Christ and blessed by God. Though the greatest benefits — complete grace and preservation from any sin from her first moment — were bestowed upon Mary, we also receive the benefits which come from Christ's Paschal Mystery.

- Mary, through her Son, was born without sin. In Baptism, we are reborn without sin: Christ frees us from sin and, through the Holy Spirit, also makes us temples of God. Filled with the grace of God and in union with the Trinity, we can grow in wisdom and faith in the present day.

- Finally, in Mary, we have both the model of the Church (all the members of Christ's body) and the model of a faith-filled disciple: "Seeking after the glory of Christ, the Church becomes more like (Mary's) lofty type, and continually progresses in faith, hope, and charity, seeking and doing the will of God in all things" (*Lumen Gentium*, No. 65).

St. Andrew of Crete really said it well for us as we consider Mary as the birthday candle of our present existence: "Justly then do we celebrate this mystery since it signifies for us a double grace.... Darkness yields before the coming of light, and grace exchanges legalism for freedom. But midway between the two stands today's mystery, at the frontier where types and symbols give way to reality, and the old is replaced by the new." [34]

Just like John's, Mary's birthday offers us a hinge moment in our history of salvation. Taking some time each year to celebrate both these hinge moments can help us better orient ourselves in our own journeys to the eternal future of our own hoped-for sainthood.

The Future

The last candle on Nana's birthday cake was for the future. It was meant to signify all our hopes and dreams for good things to come. And that is exactly what we hope for as members of Christ's Church: to follow John and Mary and all the saints into the glorious future that will mean "Sainthood now" in the eternal now.

The final of the three birthdays is the most important of all. It is even celebrated on the secular calendar. It is that of Jesus. It is also the first birthday celebrated in the Church's liturgical calendar each year — right at the end of Advent.

Clearly, the focus of Advent is on the word "coming," as in some future, but imminent, event. The dictionary tells us that "advent" derives ultimately from a Latin word (*advenire*) meaning an arrival. In ancient Rome, the word *adventus* had both a sacred and a festive meaning. An "*adventus*" was a special event. It was first used to refer to the various pagan gods, whose statues were removed from their temples each year to be freshly decorated and then returned there with great ceremony to symbolize the renewed coming of the god among the people. This celebration was called an "*adventus*."

The same sort of pageantry was eventually taken up by the Caesars — when they were considered "gods on earth" — to honor their travels throughout the empire. When Caesar came to a city for a state visit, special coins were minted and parades and events were held to mark the *adventus* of the emperor.

It doesn't take long to understand how the great celebrations of the emperor's *adventus* could take on new meaning for Roman Christians: the coming of Christ.

The actual birth of Jesus was not kept as a feast by Christians for several centuries. When it did develop, it did so around the older Roman winter feast of *Sol Invictus* — the unconquered sun — which was held on December 25. Called the *Natalis Solis Invicti* (the birth of the unconquered sun), it honored the birth of the god of the soldiers, Mithra, sometimes called Mithros or Mithras. Aspects of this midwinter feast, which also honored the sun, lent itself readily to explaining Christ as the unconquered Son of God, who had conquered death itself. *The Catholic Encyclopedia* cites St. John Chrysostom in the fourth century noting parallels between the Mithra feast and the birth of our Lord: "They call it the 'Birthday of the Unconquered.' Who indeed is so unconquered as Our Lord…? Or, if they say that it is the birthday of the sun, He is the Sun of Justice." [35]

Advent, as we know it today — while influenced by celebrations in Gaul (France and Spain) — was formalized by the Roman Church under Pope Gregory the Great (d. 604). He set the season as encompassing the four Sundays before the feast of the Nativity, the celebration of the coming of "God with us."

In Jesus, our God comes to visit us, but — unlike those early emperors — our God stays with us. He stays so that He might walk with us into the future, and into eternity.

Advent really has us looking at three candles again. Yes, there are four candles on the Advent wreath, but remember that three of them are purple: Past, future and present.

- Looking back at the events of Bethlehem, we see how our God and King came to live among us, as one of us: the Holy God-Made-Man.

- Looking forward, to the Second Coming, we can also look forward to Christ's coming in a glory that will far surpass that of any emperor of ancient Rome. "Then they will see the Son of Man coming in a cloud with power and great glory" (Luke 21:27, Gospel for First Sunday of Advent, Cycle C).

- Finally, in between these two comings — Bethlehem and the end of time — lies the time in which we live. It is here, in the present that forever unfolds into the future, that we find the importance of this birthday of Christ for us. The liturgies for Advent remind us that Christ comes into our very own lives, to each of us personally. And He comes right now, today.

As St. Charles Borromeo (d. 1584) said in a pastoral letter about Advent: "This holy season teaches us … Christ, who came once in the flesh, is prepared to come again. When we remove all obstacles to his presence, he will come, at any hour and moment, to dwell spiritually in our hearts, bringing with him the riches of his grace." [36]

The celebration of Jesus' birth seems an obvious moment of grace for the Church. Placing that celebration as we do, at the darkest and coldest time of the year (at least in the Northern Hemisphere), we emphasize that Jesus is the Word of God, the "light shining in the darkness," the One who overcame the darkness of death and the cold of the grave. Tying His birth to the day when the sun begins its long trek back toward the promise of spring made sense to the early Church of the past, around the fourth century. And it makes sense to us in the present, when each of us is on the long trek of earthly life to the spring of our future births into eternal life with Jesus. The celebration of Christmas gives us a very bright candle on which we can fix our eyes, looking with hope to the future.

Discussion/Reflection:

1. Does your family have any birthday traditions that celebrate the past, present, or future of someone's life?

2. How do you celebrate the heavenly birthdays of friends and family who have passed away?

3. Christmas celebrations help remind us of God's presence in natural events like the change of seasons. What other Christian feasts have logical ties to nature events that could have been useful in spreading the Gospel message to people who have never heard of Christianity?

CHAPTER EIGHT

"What's in a Name?"

Patron Saints

While our birthday candles from the last chapter are still burning brightly, let's look at another reason to throw a party.

Besides candles, most of us celebrate birthdays with presents and special food. But we could continue the celebration because there's another day for us to celebrate besides the day on which we were born: it's our name day. Yet, how many of us even know that we have a name day, or when it is?

Well, if you have any Eastern European heritage in your background, you probably have celebrated your name day. For example, in the Czech Republic, the event is called *svátek* or *jmeniny* (which roughly translates as "holiday"). It is more common to celebrate name days in areas of the Eastern Orthodox Church, such as Greece or Russia, but it is not unheard of across many part of Europe. In Spanish-speaking countries, the celebration is called *día del santo*. And even in Italy, you see some people celebrating their *l'onomástico* as if it were a second birthday.

So what's a name day? Name days celebrate our baptismal names — or, more correctly, they celebrate the Christian names we received at Baptism. These are most often the names of saints, but they can also be derivations of holy events as is the case for the name "Anastasia," which is originally a Greek name referring to the "resurrection."

Name days are usually celebrated on the feast days of the saints who share our names, not on our birthdays. (That brings

us to the part about having another reason to party on an entirely separate day of the year.)

As we said, not everyone receives a saint's name when
they are born. While most of the top 20 baby names listed by
the U.S. Social Security Administration for the census year of
2010 seem to have Christian — or at least Biblical — connec-
tions, not all are as readily apparent as Jacob, or Sophia (which
comes from the Greek word for wisdom). For example, one
might not think that 2010's number-eight girls' name — Madison — had any connection to a Christian name. Yet "Madison"
is sometimes listed as deriving from "Mad's son" with "Mad"
being a diminutive of Matthew, like Jimmy is of James. So all
the Madisons out there have ties to an evangelist Apostle, the
one who was once a tax collector and who, by the way, hosted a
dinner party for Jesus.

People with names such as "Star" or "Butler" might need
to look to their middle names to find a saint to use for their
name days. Most of us, though, can turn to our baptismal names
to find our name day. While it's not required by the Church —
canon law only says that "parents, sponsors, and the pastor are
to take care that a name foreign to Christian sensibility is not
given" (canon 855) — most parents still work in a saint's name
for their child's baptism.

What's with the Church asking parents not to choose a
name "foreign to church sensibility?" Yes, there really are some
names that might be best avoided. A good example appeared in
the news from New Zealand in the summer of 2011. That July,
the national Registrar of Births, Deaths, and Marriages banned
"Lucifer" as an accepted baby name. (It also banned names like
"Bishop" and "King," which are probably better for horses or dogs
anyway.) Lucifer would certainly qualify as violating canon 855.

So what if your given name — or even your middle name
— doesn't seem to fit a saint's feast? Well, don't feel left out. Re-

member the early Christians. Since most early Christians were baptized as adults, not all of them came with Christian names from birth. And not all of them changed their Roman or Greek names once they became Christian. However, many early Christians did choose to be known by a new name, in honor of a saint — often a martyr. For example, *The Catholic Encyclopedia* cites the *Acts of St. Balsamus* (Balsamus was martyred in A.D. 331) as showing a connection between being baptized (and confirmed since that was done at the same time in the early Church) and a new name: "By my paternal name I am called Balsamus, but by the spiritual name, which I received in Baptism, I am known as Peter." [37]

From this we can see that it's not only Baptism, but also Confirmation, that can give us ways to acquire a name day saint. After all, for Confirmation we are asked to select a saint whom we might wish to emulate when we approach this sacrament.

And, if you need another source for a saint's name, there are also patron saints to consider. While one's patron saint is usually one's name day saint, that's not always the case.

The word "patron" comes from the Latin *patronus* which derives from "father." In ancient Rome, a patron was someone who became your legal advocate. Early Roman senators had the title of *patronus*, as did the former owners of slaves who became freed. A *patronus* was obligated to help you. But the obligation worked both ways — while the *patronus* protected you and looked out for your interests, you were also expected to give financial support to that *patronus*.

Our patron saints help us too — be they our name saints from birth or a saint who came into our lives later. Patron saints act as intercessors to God. In this, they imitate Christ, our perfect Intercessor. The saints, through their lives, have shown us how to be Christ-like. Now, through their prayers, they strengthen us in following the path of Christ.

There are many types of patron saints. For example, there are patron saints of countries and of dioceses. These are often designated because the patron lived, died, or was buried there. So St. Francis of Assisi and St. Catherine of Siena are patrons of Italy. A patron may also be named because of a special tie to an area: the patroness of Mexico is Mary, under the title of Our Lady of Guadalupe, because of the famous apparition there in 1531.

There are also patron saints for occupations. Many times, the patron saint practiced this profession. So St. Joseph is the patron of carpenters, while the patron of homemakers is St. Anne, the mother of the Blessed Virgin. And it's not just the occupations we might think of as everyday jobs: there is a patron for pawnbrokers (St. Nicholas), for playing card manufacturers (St. Balthazar, one of the Magi), and for junk dealers (St. Sebastian).

Not only human saints are chosen as patrons. Angels like Michael and Raphael are patrons of soldiers and healers, respectively. And there are specific aspects of some of the great saints that qualify them as patrons. So a saint like Mother Mary is the patron of schools, churches, groups, and countries in various ways: as the Immaculate Conception, she is the patron of the United States and as Our Lady of the Hurons, she is the patron of Canada.

Even the various human aspects of Christ — the Sacred Heart, the Holy Name, the Holy Childhood, and the Resurrection to name a few — are called upon for assistance. The relics of Christ's Passion — such as the Holy Cross and the Crown of Thorns — serve as patrons for parishes and hospitals.

So each of us has at least one patron saint we can use for a name day:

- the saint whose name we received when we were baptized;
- the saint whose name we chose when we were confirmed;
- the patron of our professions;

- even the patrons of our hobbies — for example, St. Hubert is the patron of hunters.

Some people even choose a new patron saint each year. For example, Maria Von Trapp, of *The Sound of Music* fame, wrote about how her family would choose patron saints each Advent.

"The family meets on Saturday evening, and with the help of the missal and a book called *The Martyrology*, which lists thousands of saints as they are celebrated throughout the year, they choose as many new saints as there are members of the household," Trapp wrote in her 1955 book, *Around the Year with the Trapp Family*. She added that they sometimes chose saints according to themes — such as martyrs. After the names were chosen for the year, the family calligrapher would artistically write down each saint's name and then hand the listings over to the mother of the house, who would choose a saint for each family member. [38]

St. Faustina Kowalska, who led the church to the Divine Mercy devotion, knew a similar custom in her convent of the Sisters of Our Lady of Mercy in Krakow, Poland. She wrote about it in her diary, *Divine Mercy in My Soul*.

"There is a custom among us of drawing by lot, on New Year's Day, special Patrons for ourselves for the whole year.... When we came to refectory for breakfast, we blessed ourselves and began drawing our patrons. When I approached the holy cards on which the names of the patrons were written, without hesitation I took one, but I didn't read the name immediately." [39]

Her patron for that year — 1935 — was the Most Blessed Eucharist, one of the titles of Christ.

A modern spin on this custom of choosing patron saints each year can be found at many Catholic blogs and religious education websites. Some sites will even help you choose a patron saint for yourself — some by using a random generator program, while others use lists of saints' attributes to match an appropriate saint with you after you have shared a little about your personal interests or prayer concerns.

It's never too late to choose a patron saint — a saint whose day you could honor as your name day. Taking someone's name shows a special commitment to living a Christian life as exemplified by the life of our patron — that's why we take a new name at Confirmation.

Not only do patron saints intercede for us with God, but God also uses them and all the saints to act directly in our lives. They are examples, guides, and inspirations for us. It is through his saints — whether still alive today or alive in Christ — that God speaks to us.

The framers of the Second Vatican Council reminded us of God's work through the saints when they wrote, "God shows to men, in a vivid way, his presence and his face in the lives of those companions of ours in the human condition who are more perfectly transformed into the image of Christ. He speaks to us in them and offers us a sign of the kingdom" (*Lumen Gentium*, No. 50).

Patron saints add their prayers to ours when we approach God. For our part, we honor their memories and invite them to share in our celebrations of faith. They do this through the union we call the Communion of Saints. All members of Christ's Church — both in this world and the next — share in this communion. St. Paul in the First letter to the Corinthians explained this communion: "If one member suffers, all the members suffer with it; if one member is honored, all the members share its joy" (1 Cor 12:26).

Inviting the saints to share in the parties we have for our name days is one way to let them share in our joy. After all, they are with us and care about us. Why wouldn't they want to be part of our parties? Don't they want to help us get to be part of the biggest party of all, the Eternal Banquet? There they wait, ready to toast us with the cry, "*Santo subito!*"

So, how about a toast to St. Patrick?

Discussion/Reflection:

1. Who is your patron saint? (Remember, you can have more than one patron saint.)

2. Is there a story behind how your baptismal name, or your confirmation name, was chosen?

3. Think about the definition of the word "patron." What new insights does that definition give you into your relationship with your patron saint?

4. Think of your patron saint and decide one way you might honor him or her at a party for your name day. For example, place roses on the table if your name is Mary or any variation on the name of the Blessed Mother.

CHAPTER NINE

"Doesn't He Just Glow?"

Saints' Symbols

Who's that man standing in the shadows in the corner of the darkened church?

Well, it might not be in a corner. It could be on a stained glass window. Or maybe he's standing in a painting in the side chapel.

There are many ways to represent saints of the Church — not just our patron saints, but any holy person of Christ's Church. We see them in windows, statues, and on prayer cards. But there are so many saints and blesseds that it can be hard to tell which saint is which, even when we're looking right at them.

In our media age, certain saints are easy to spot: there are photographs of St. Thérèse of Lisieux, old movie footage of Padre Pio (St. Pio of Pietrelcina), and plenty of news videos of Mother Teresa and Pope John Paul II.

However, most saints and blesseds lived on earth long before there were cameras. Yet we readily recognize their images, thanks to the repetition of symbols associated with each of them. As they say, "a picture is worth a thousand words."

A symbol always connects us with a story. For example, there are many representations of Jesus: with a beard and without, as a child, as a baby, as a man, and even as a shepherd. There is Jesus with black hair or blond hair, Jesus with dark skin or blue eyes. And yet, we still recognize all of these images as Jesus. Why? Because there's a cross halo above Him. Or the cross itself with Him. Or a crown of thorns. Or a lamb. Or He has two fingers raised in a blessing that shows His human and divine nature. And then there's that look in His eyes.

All these symbols remind us of who Jesus is and what He has done. They remind us of who Jesus was for His saints and who He is for each of us. The symbols of the saints also remind us of this and tap into stories that are etched in our own hearts because they speak to us of Jesus.

There are many symbols for the saints. Some are common to many saints or symbolize certain characteristics of a group of saints. For example:

- Martyrs are often shown carrying a palm branch — an ancient sign of victory and a reminder of the verse in the Book of Revelation about those "who have survived the time of great distress" (7:14).

- Virgins are shown in white attire for purity, or with a lamb or a crown of flowers — such as St. Agnes, whose name is similar to the Latin *agnus* for lamb, is likely to be shown with a lamb.

- Books are part of teaching, so many great teachers of the Church are shown holding books — such as the evangelists and saints like St. Teresa of Ávila, a doctor of the Church.

- If a saint is shown holding a church, it means he or she founded a church, a diocese, or an abbey. Art historians trace this back to at least the building of St. Vitale Church in Ravenna, Italy, in the sixth century. In its dome is an image of Christ (beardless) with a representation of Bishop Ecclesio — who founded St. Vitale's — holding a church. Churches are held also by Sts. Jerome, Ambrose, Clotilde, and the brother saints, Cyril and Methodius.

- Crowns often symbolize earthly rulership as well as heavenly reward and are seen on St. Elizabeth of Hungary (a queen), St. Helen (an empress), and St. Louis IX (a king.)

- Shells symbolize pilgrims and are seen with St. James the Greater, St. Augustine, and St. Bridget. (A shell is also a symbol of St. John the Baptist.)

- Lilies are another sign of the pure of heart and are shown with saints like the Virgin Mary, Joseph, Anthony of Padua, and Kateri Tekakwitha, "the Lily of the Mohawks."

Many saints who founded or belonged to religious orders are shown garbed in that order's distinctive religious habit. So St. Francis of Assisi wears the grey (earliest habit) or brown robes of the Franciscans, as do Lawrence of Brindisi and Clare of Assisi (founder of the Poor Clares). Dominic, Catherine of Siena and Rose of Lima all wear Dominican black over white. Carmelites like St. John of the Cross and Blessed Elizabeth of the Holy Trinity wear their order's distinctive white over black. And Blessed Mother Teresa wears her Missionaries of Charity's white sari with its blue stripes.

While many common symbols identify common aspects of saints, there are certain symbols that pinpoint specific saints. So we see:

- A green shamrock for St. Patrick, who evangelized Ireland, the Emerald Isle;

- The wheel on which she was martyred for Catherine of Alexandra;

- The many arrows protruding from Sebastian's body;

- Keys in the hands of Peter;

- Denis holding his decapitated head under his arm;

- The hunter saint, Hubert, and his stag;

- Francis and the wolf of Gubbio;

- Thérèse and her armful of roses;

- George with his dragon;

- Andrew with his X-shaped cross;

- John the Baptist in his camel-hair robe;

- Mary Magdalene and her egg. (Egg? A tradition of her later life associates red eggs — perhaps the start of the Easter egg custom — with Mary's preaching of the Gospel of the Risen Christ to the Emperor Tiberius in Rome.)

The most common symbol of all for saints, of course, is the halo, that special glow that speaks to us of heaven. A halo — whether around an animal (like a dove or a lamb) or the head of an angel — immediately tells us three things:

- This is the image of an important, if not divine, person;

- We're seeing the depiction of an important, if not supernatural, event;

- There's a lesson here about deeply held religious beliefs.

We're used to seeing halos used as Christian religious symbols. Religious symbols work like stop signs — they alert us to the fact that we need to pay attention to something important. However, placing rings around the heads of people or objects is not something Christians invented. Ancient religions often represented deities or sovereigns in this way. For example, Egyptian art shows gods crowned with sun disks. In fact, the word "halo" derives from the Greek word "*halos*" (disk of the sun), which came from the name of the all-seeing sun god, Helios.

To the ancients, the sun was the center of the universe. It gave warmth, caused grain to grow, brought light to darkness, and — as spring and the planting season approached — brought life to what had seemed dead. The sun ruled the heavens — greater than the moon, stars, and planets. To depict the sun was to depict power and authority. To show kings and gods with halos told people that they had similar importance.

So it's not surprising, with these ties to other, pagan religions, that early depictions of Christ did *not* show Him with a halo. Instead, He was shown with the Cross or with His fingers raised in blessing. However, since the symbolism was so well known, the artistic embellishment of halos began to appear in Christian art by the third century. Once Christianity became an officially accepted state religion under the Roman emperor Constantine in the fourth century, such depictions became common.

Even so, early halos were used for Jesus only when He was shown enthroned, exalted as the Christ, the Anointed One of God. Only later was the halo used in representations of His earthly life.

By the fifth century, halos became acceptable in all religious art, not only for Jesus, but also for Mary, angels, saints, and various animals (lambs, doves, fish). This adoption of halos from ancient art shows a shift in theological emphasis. Non-Christian art had used halos to signify majesty and power. Christian art began to use halos to show the presence of God's grace — the ultimate majesty and power.

However, as halos began to be used not only for Christ, but for every saint, angel, and even a few animals (think doves and lambs here), questions arose as to how to signify the differences in what these halos represented. For example, while Jesus is divine, Mary is not. Thus, different halos — besides the familiar round or ring-shaped ones — developed to represent different things:

- **Triangular** — used only to represent a member of the Trinity. So a lamb carried by St. Agnes will look different than the Lamb of God.

- **Aureole** — a glow surrounding the entire body. First used only to represent the Divine, it was later extended to Mary to represent her special relationship with God.

- **Rainbow aureole** — God spoke to Noah about His "bow in the clouds" (Gen 9:13), and the prophet Ezekiel saw a vision of God's throne surrounded by a rainbow (see Ez 1:28). The rainbow also reflects the glory that surrounds God's throne, as noted in Revelation 4:3, and has most often been used only for God, for the Holy Spirit, and for Jesus when His divinity is being emphasized.

- **Cruciform halo** — A cross in the center of a halo usually represents Christ, but can also represent any member of the Trinity. (So a dove shone in artwork of Jesus' Baptism might have a triangular or cruciform halo, and the fingers of God reaching down from heaven, while usually surrounded by a triangle of light, may also have a halo with the Cross' shape.)

- **Fish-shaped** — This is a more solid shape surrounding the body, such as that seen in the image of Our Lady of Guadalupe. It is sometimes called the *mandorla* from the Italian word for "almond." Its resemblance to a fish bladder — it is also called *vesica piscis* — is a reminder of one of the earliest symbols of Christ: the fish. The fish is a play on words — an acrostic — of Jesus' name in Greek: Jesus Christ, Son of God, Savior, or ICTHYS (Iēsous Christos, Theou Yios, Sōtēr). The almond-shape to the fish halo serves to represent the complete bond of the saint's life to Christ.

- **Shield** — This depicts the presence of God protecting the saint's life.

- **Square** — A square halo, rarely seen, represents a living person. Several popes allowed representations of themselves as pope shown with square halos. This can be seen in the Roman church of San Marco, which was rebuilt by Pope Gregory IV in 833. He is represented in the apse mosaics with a square halo.

- **Blue halos** — represent heaven, another link to God.

- **Gold halos** — This color represents both eternity, since gold does not tarnish, and royalty, since it was the metal of kings.

So whatever the symbol for a saint, and whatever type of glow surrounds him or her, there is always an underlying message: These people were like us and now they are like Christ — whom we recognize instantly in His portraits. The saints lived in the knowledge and ways of Christ and now they shine as models for us. As the *Catechism of the Catholic Church* explains, "the saints show the power of the Spirit alive within the church and sustain the hope of believers through their example and intercession" (CCC 826).

So when you next see a statue and recognize a particular saint, it's because you remember the story of how they showed Christ to others. In the same way, we are called to be stories of Christ to others. As Pope Paul VI said, "the life of each individual child of God is joined in Christ and through Christ by a wonderful link to the life of all his other Christian brothers and sisters." [40]

Discussion/Reflection:

1. What's your favorite saint symbol?

2. All of us have the goal of sainthood. If your name were ever entered into the calendar of saints, what symbol would you think would be used to represent you?

3. What saint do you always recognize by their symbol?

CHAPTER TEN

The "Show and Tell" Saints

Doctors of the Church

Remember "Show and Tell"?

Back in grade school, "Show and Tell" meant getting up in front of class to describe or explain something you had brought from home. It had to be something important, maybe even something that was part of your family history.

I didn't often do well with Show and Tell. Once I brought a rock from Yellowstone Park. I might have received a "B" for that.

Imagine if I had stood up in front of class one day and presented — God. That would have aced the project for the whole year!

Well, in a manner of speaking, that's exactly what a Doctor of the Church does: "Show and Tell" God.

While there are thousands of saints in the Catholic Church, there are only thirty-five "Doctors of the Universal Church." Consider them as our "super saints." Super superheroes, if you will.

The title "Doctor of the Universal Church" identifies a saint as a theologian of the greatest degree. Surprisingly, when looking up the word "doctor" in Webster's Dictionary, the first definition does not deal with medical practice, but with theology. A "doctor" is listed as "an eminent theologian," or one who has studied God.

Since all doctors of the church are saints — although all saints are not doctors — we can guess that each Doctor lived close to God, intent upon being shown God's ways and eventually revealing (telling) those ways to others.

The newest Doctor of the Church, Hildegard of Bingen, was never formally canonized by the Church. When Pope Benedict XVI intended to formally declare her a Doctor of the Church on October 7, 2012, he decided to declare Hildegard to be a saint by a process called "equivalent canonization" on May 10, 2012. This is a judgment that can be made by the pope regarding the holiness of the life of one who is already called a Servant of God. "Equivalent canonization" dates to the papacy of Benedict XIV (1740–58) and is another example of the privilege that popes have when it comes to declaring saints. Benedict XVI's action not only recognized a case of *Santo subito*, a long-standing church tradition that honored Hildegard's sanctity (she died in 1179), it also cleared the way for him to declare her a Doctor of the Church.

Doctors of the Church are experts at "show and tell." The word "doctor" comes from the Latin verb, *docēre*, meaning "to teach, show or inform." This is what Doctors of the Church do best: teach us about God and show us how to live a Christian life. That, in fact, lays out for us the three norms followed when selecting a person as a Doctor of the Church:

- All Doctors are canonized, that is, saints. This means that we know that, in the past, they led holy lives and, right now, they're in the presence of God and interceding for us on earth.

- All were authorities, in their own ways, regarding matters of belief and of the Church, and made important contributions to our repository of faith.

- We recognize them as reliable teachers of the Faith.

Originally, Doctors of the Church were not officially declared as such, but were simply honored in our tradition as prominent teachers of the faith. It wasn't until the end of the thirteenth century that the title "Doctor of the Church" was officially bestowed. It went immediately to four great teachers of the Western Church: Ambrose, Jerome, Augustine, and Gregory the Great. St. Thomas Aquinas followed in 1568. Prior to this, in the Eastern Christian Church, three saints were honored as "*Hierarchs* (meaning 'of sacred authority') of the Church" from the ninth century, so declared by the Byzantine Emperor Leo VI the Wise. There is also an ancient feast in the Byzantine Catholic Church, dating to at least the eleventh century, for the Three Hierarchs, celebrated on January 30. The Three Hierarchs are Basil the Great, Gregory of Nazianzus, and John Chrysostom.

Not long after Thomas Aquinas was honored as a Doctor of the Church, people realized that it was not only the teachings of Western saints that had been of extreme value in the development of Church Tradition. So Pope St. Pius V declared that four Eastern saints were also Doctors of the Universal Church in 1568: they were the Three Hierarchs, Basil, Gregory of Nazianzus, and John Chrysostom, along with St. Athanasius.

Yet being a saint, or a hierarch, or a bishop, or a preacher does not automatically assure that someone will be declared a Doctor of the Church. Many great saints and spiritual guides — such as Francis of Assisi, Gregory of Nyssa, and Dominic — are not Doctors of the Church (though they could well be named so someday).

The rarity of Doctors of the Church is seen both in their small numbers (there are only thirty-five of them) and the fact that there was a big gap between the naming of St. Gregory the Great in 1298 and the naming of the next Doctor of the Church in 1568. (This was St. Thomas Aquinas.) Why such a time gap? And why have only thirty-five been declared so far? And why not someone like St. Thomas More, who was a great leader, or St. Francis Xavier or St. Patrick, who were great missionaries, or St. Clare, the founder of the Poor Clares and a patron of television? Were they poor teachers? Did they lack sufficient knowledge of the Faith? Did they not "Show and Tell" God well enough to others?

Of course not.

When we look both at the writings of the Doctors of the Church and at the times during which they were declared Doctors, we may gain some insights to answer these questions.

From the time of the Roman emperor Constantine in the fourth century until the sixteenth century, the Church occupied a fairly unchallenged place in world culture and history. All that changed, however, when Martin Luther posted his theological protests on that Wittenburg church door in 1517 and lit the powder keg that became the Protestant Revolution.

St. Thomas Aquinas became a Doctor of the Church in 1568, during what was a turbulent time — both in the social world and in faith life. The Wars of Religion raged in France (1562–98) and Calvinism was on the rise in Scotland, Switzerland, the Netherlands, England, and France. Against this backdrop, Thomas Aquinas was honored.

Why? Well, in his day, Thomas Aquinas strongly defended the Faith against those who championed the teachings of Aristotle, a pagan philosopher. Also Aquinas' *Summa Theologica* — even unfinished as it is — is considered the greatest single writing on the Christian Faith, showing and telling a marvelous defense of all that the Church teaches and believes.

Looking at things through the lens of his time, it becomes easier to see why Pope St. Pius V might have felt 1568 was a good time to declare the first new Doctor of the Church in nearly 300 years — and why he chose St. Thomas Aquinas. The Eastern Doctors were added that same year, perhaps to emphasize the universal nature of the Church.

In 1588, Pope Sixtus V named the next Doctor: St. Bonaventure. Bonaventure, a minister-general of the Franciscan order, was responsible for so much reform and revitalization in his religious community that he is called its second founder. Pope Sixtus was also undertaking vast reforms in his day, both of the Roman Curia and the College of Cardinals. His reforms remained essentially unchanged until the Second Vatican Council opened in 1962. So Sixtus probably felt an affinity with St. Bonaventure the reformer, and wanted to hold him up as a model for what Sixtus himself was doing.

So it may well be that Doctors of the Church are named at times when their writings and teachings seem particularly relevant to the Church. Some Doctors of the Church have even more titles that tell us something about their "Show and Tell" expertise. For example, St. Alphonsus Liguori, founder of the Redemptorist Order, was named a Doctor of the Church in 1871 and is also called "Doctor Most Zealous." Alphonsus was a writer — 111 spiritual works — a bishop, a composer, a lawyer, and a missionary to poor young people. During his first years of priesthood, he founded Evening Chapels of Prayer, run by lay leaders in poor communities. Clearly, Alphonsus was a very zealous man. Pope Pius IX named Alphonsus a Doctor in 1871, the time of the First Vatican Council, which addressed papal infallibility, but which also had to be suspended because of the invasion of Rome during the Franco-Prussian War. (That war eventually led to the end of the Papal States as a geographic and political entity.)

Another time of change, both secular and within the Church, was the 1970s. Both St. Teresa of Ávila and St. Catherine of Siena were declared Doctors in 1970 (the first two women so honored). The 1970s were the years of concern for women's voices throughout society. These were also the first years of the reforms following Vatican II. Both Catherine and

Teresa were dynamic reformers. Teresa returned her Carmelite order to its original austerity, revitalizing it and founding new convents. Catherine helped end the Avignon Papacy and return the pope to Rome. She also worked to end the Western Schism that had erupted in the late 1370s.

Catherine of Sienna only lived 33 years and was possibly illiterate — she used secretaries to dictate her many letters. Even Pope Paul VI, in declaring her a Doctor of the Church on October 4, 1970, called her "the uncultured virgin of Fontebranda" whose theology was "bare of any scientific clothing." Yet Catherine is accounted as one of the Church's great mystics and spiritual guides. As Paul VI also said, she showed "infused wisdom" that came from the gift of the Holy Spirit. [41]

It was the same in the case of St. Thérèse of Lisieux. Only 24 when she died, Thérèse was no scholar. Yet her *Story of a Soul* has guided countless people along her "Little Way" to God since her death in 1897. In declaring her a Doctor of the Church on October 19, 1997, the brink of a new millennium, Pope John Paul II said Thérèse taught a "science of love." In fact, she is called "the Doctor of Love."

Like Catherine, Thérèse was not greatly educated. "In the writings of Thérèse of Lisieux, we do not find perhaps, as in other doctors, a scholarly presentation of the things of God," Pope John Paul II said, "but we can discern an enlightened witness of faith which … reveals the mystery and holiness of the Church."

Thérèse's "Little Way" involved complete trust in God, the trust exemplified by little ones — by children who love Show and Tell games. She also professed a great love for — and a belief that she was being greatly loved by — Jesus. All this happened at a time in the Church and the world (she died on September 30, 1897, the brink of another millennium) when Jesus was commonly viewed as remote, a divine presence at the altar — not as a close, personal, and beloved friend. When he named Thérèse a Doctor of the Church, Pope John Paul was also calling for a renewed understanding of Jesus as the world neared the 2,000th anniversary of his birth. No doubt, Thérèse's example helped with that.

Of course, many of the Doctors of the Church *were* highly educated. The title of "doctor," when it was first given in the late Middle Ages (around the fourteenth century), referred to someone with an advanced degree of education, such as law, the arts, medicine, or theology, which were all expanding in popularity. Something more like what a Ph.D. title means today. As noted, this doctorate title, then and now, did not refer to medicine. The people who dealt with medicine in the Middle Ages were more commonly called "healers," "herbalists," or even "leeches" (called that because they used them). Yet they, too, were masters in their own way — the way of plants and folk remedies, many of which did indeed later find their way into the world of medicine (including leeches).

Hildegard of Bingen, the most recent Doctor of the Church, was in fact a healer in her day, and quite educated. Having been sickly as a child, she later studied and wrote extensively about herbal medicine. She was also a Benedictine prioress, visionary, composer of hymns, and even invented an alternative alphabet. Speaking about Hildegard in 2010, Pope Benedict XVI cited John Paul's reference to "the feminine genius which had appeared in the course of history, in the midst of all peoples and nations." [43]

Hildegard, Pope Benedict said, "manifests the versatility of interests and cultural vivacity of the female monasteries of the Middle Ages" and remains an example to this day.

> "With the spiritual authority with which she was endowed, in the last years of her life, Hildegard set out on

journeys, despite her advanced age and the uncomfortable conditions of travel, in order to speak to the people of God. They all listened willingly, even when she spoke severely: they considered her a messenger sent by God." [44]

Hildegard's variety of gifts and her defense of the Church have much to "Show and Tell" the Church of the twenty-first century, as Pope Benedict realized. In her appointment as a super saint, we can see yet another example of how the popes have used the saints to Show and Tell us about God in the classrooms of everyday life.

Discussion/Reflection:

1. Who is your "Show and Tell" saint — even if he or she isn't a Doctor of the Church?

2. There are only four female Doctors of the Church. If you could decide on another female Doctor of the Church, who would you choose? What special gifts would this woman offer to the Church at this time in history?

3. Which Doctor(s) of the Church are you most familiar with? (See Appendix I for list.)

CHAPTER ELEVEN

Getting Lost in the Crowd

Veneration of Saints

Patron saints. Name saints. Apostles, martyrs, confessors. Doctors of the Church.

Have you ever been lost in a crowd? All that pushing and shoving. The press of people, the push of bodies, the sound of countless voices. It can be overwhelming. Especially if you don't know where you're going. Even worse if you're a stranger, or you don't speak the language.

That's what often happens when we speak with others about "praying to the saints." Part of the difficulty with understanding what we Catholics are doing when we "pray to the saints" goes back to understanding what "pray to" means. In our modern understanding of the phrase "pray to," we immediately associate it with the word "prayer," which is an act of worship. And worship, for Catholics as well as other Christians, *is* directed only to God.

Confusion abounds. The Catholic Church, to help with that, actually has special terms: *Dulia* and *latria*. Both come from the Greek and were the subject of much debate by early leaders of the Church, such as St. Augustine. He defined them, respectively, as obedience (*dulia*) and homage (*latria*).

Both words have to do with honor and worship. But *dulia* (which means "service" or "servitude") has to do with the honor one gives to another human being — even though it sometimes meant the honor which a slave gave to a master. *Dulia* is also the honor which we give to saints. We do so because they have gone before us and, if we ask for their help, they are able to show us the way through the crowd. (The Church has another term — *hyperdulia* — which is reserved for Mary alone, sort of a "super-servitude" to the "Mother of my Lord." It's part of the reason we call Mary, "Our Lady," just in the same way that knights of earthly kingdoms might address a queen.)

Latria, on the other hand, always refers to the divine and to the honor given only to God. For this, we have the example of the angels and the saints in heaven as is shown to us in the Book of Revelation: "They prostrated themselves before the throne, worshiped God, and exclaimed: 'Amen. Blessings and glory, wisdom and thanksgiving, honor, power and might be to our God forever and ever. Amen'" (Rev 7:11–12).

Without a clear understanding of the meaning of our acts — much less our words — it can all get mixed up. With all the prayers, worship, veneration, and honor being tossed around in Catholic circles, people watching from the outside (and even some of us on the inside) can get confused. In fact, these less-than-clear understandings of what we are doing when we pray became part of the confusion between the Catholic Church and Protestant reformers, such as John Calvin, who wrote, "It is idolatrous to worship in any degree any of the angels or so-called saints who have died." [45] Martin Luther's *Large Catechism* roundly condemned — in sarcastic terms — the idea of focusing on one's own personal saint for help, to the exclusion of turning to God: "If anyone had (a) toothache, he fasted and honored St. Apollonia;... if he was afraid of fire, he chose St. Lawrence as his helper in need; if he dreaded pestilence, he made a vow to St. Sebastian or Rochio." [46]

Luther, of course, was trained as a Catholic priest and knew better than most what was supposed to be going on. And remember that he never denied the existence of saints, especially the Communion of Saints. No, Luther's concern was that "all these (people intensely praying to saints) place their heart and trust elsewhere than in the true God, look for nothing good to Him nor seek it from Him." [47]

Every Catholic has heard a variation of this concern: "Why do you pray to saints?" "Aren't you worshiping Mary?" "Aren't those statues of saints in your church idolatrous?" "We don't need anyone but Jesus."

As we said earlier, we all agree that prayer is directed only to God, because we worship only God. However, when we are talking about saints, we need to understand "pray to" not as being the same thing as the word "prayer" but as being most closely related to the word "pray." The word "pray" comes from various words; in Old English, French, Latin, German, and even Sanskrit, they all mean "to ask."

When we pray to the saints, we are *asking* for their help. Maybe using the phrase "pray with" instead of "pray to" would make matters easier. After all, we aren't saying, "St. Michael, heal me!" Or "St. Francis, forgive my sins." We know those things are God's venue alone, not the saints'. They, like everyone else who cares about us, are not divine beings; they are human like us. In fact, they are experts at being human. As such, they are there to help. They are there to guide us and give us directions to help us get through the push and shove of life.

When you are sick, or have some big problem in your life, don't you ask your friends to pray for you? Why? Because we need other people.

Jesus himself *told* us to ask others to pray for us, and with us, by joining together in prayer: "Where two or three are gathered together in my name, there am I in the midst of them" (Matt 18:20).

We believe that shared prayer is not just more powerful and more supportive than individual prayer (and remember that "individual prayer" really doesn't happen, since we are always joined together in the Body of Christ), but we also believe that shared prayer is a great act of worship and devotion to God. That is why we gather together to celebrate the Mass and for other forms of communal prayer, such as the Liturgy of the Hours, where we also offer prayers of petition. We believe that God calls us into community, so that we can share God's graces with each other.

We are the People of God and, as God's people, we join together to be with God and each other, offering praise and worship to God together, and presenting our needs and concerns — together. And that one community, gathered together in prayer, includes the saints, whom we believe are in the presence of God — right now.

The Fathers of Vatican II reminded us of this in their document on the Church, *Lumen Gentium*; in fact, they spoke about sharing prayer with the saints in terms of a journey:

> For just as Christian communion among wayfarers brings us closer to Christ, so our companionship with the saints joins us to Christ.... It is supremely fitting, therefore, that we love those friends and coheirs of Jesus Christ, who are also our brothers and extraordinary benefactors, that we render due thanks to God for them and "suppliantly invoke them and have recourse to their prayers, their power, and help in obtaining benefits from God through His Son, Jesus Christ, who is our Redeemer and Savior." For every genuine testimony of love shown by us to those in heaven, by its very nature, tends toward and terminates in Christ.... (*Lumen Gentium*, No. 50)

So the next time you feel lost in the crowd, or without directions or even any understanding of the right words to use, remember that the saints — those in heaven, right now, with

Jesus — are a part of that crowd. And they know how to speak your language better than anybody.

Discussion/Reflection:

1. Have you ever been told that you "worship" Mary or the saints? How did you answer?

2. How do you explain to children or teenagers why you pray to the saints?

3. Do you have statues or medals of any saint? Why is having an image of a saint important to you? How does it help your prayer life?

4. Do you have a favorite prayer to or by a saint?

CHAPTER TWELVE

"Holy Heaven and Holy Purgatory"

All Saints and All Souls

There are almost 7,000 saints listed in the Roman Martyrology. Talk about a crowd.

To simplify things a little, we try to provide some focus with our prayers and feast days. So, for example, there is the Litany of Saints, a prayer of petition which lists about four dozen saints by name, grouped in categories, starting with Mary, the Mother of God. Following her are the archangels and angels, and then a bit of a chronology of saints, starting with St. John the Baptist and St. Joseph, and then "all holy patriarchs and prophets" — which is a nod back to those holy ones of Old Testament times. Next come the Twelve Apostles, listed by name, the martyrs, bishops, founders of religious orders, and broad categories of saints ranging from "all you holy innocents" through "holy monks and hermits" to "holy virgins and widows." All are asked to "pray for us."

The Litany of Saints can be used in various liturgical celebrations of the Church, but the one time of year we are almost certain to hear it — even if only in the form of a hymn — is on the Feast of All Saints, November 1. The Collect (gathering prayer) for that day's Mass asks, "Almighty ever-living God, by whose gift we venerate in one celebration the merits of all the Saints, bestow on us, we pray, through the prayers of so many intercessors, an abundance of the reconciliation with you for which we earnestly long."

A feast day commemorating the saints in one all-encompassing group goes far back into Christian history. It arose from feasts honoring the martyrs, those first formally acknowledged saints. For a while, the first Sunday after Pentecost was the preferred day for a feast honoring all the saints. However, in A.D. 610, that changed. That year, Pope Boniface IV gained possession of the Roman Pantheon, an ancient Roman temple dedicated to "all the gods." Boniface had it converted into a Christian church. The Pantheon — with its architecturally famous open dome — was originally built (and rebuilt in A.D. 125) to honor the vast array of Roman deities. When Pope Boniface received the Pantheon from the Byzantine Emperor Phocas, he followed an already common tradition of rededicating pagan temples for Christian use. So Boniface dedicated the Pantheon to Mary and to the growing pantheon of Christian martyrs. It is now called *Santa Maria dei Martiri* (St. Mary of the Martyrs). Informally, the building is known as "*Santa Maria della Rotunda*" because of its round dome.

The day of the new church's dedication, May 13, 610, was a carefully chosen date. In imperial Rome, May 9, 10, and 13 were the days of *Lemuria*, a festival held to appease the gods. So not only did Pope Boniface want to re-engineer a pagan temple into a Christian church, he also wanted to re-engineer a pagan holiday of fear into a feast of joy honoring the Church's saints.

The May 13 date for All Saints' Day continued until the time of Pope Gregory III (731–41). Pope Gregory had to deal with iconoclasts, those who opposed the use of all religious icons as a form of idolatry and who destroyed many images of Christ and the saints. Pope Gregory finally excommunicated them. And, perhaps to make the message even more plain, he dedicated a chapel in St. Peter's Basilica to "all the saints" on November 1. The feast day's date has stuck ever since.

Of course, that's not the only version of why we use November 1 as the feast day of All Saints that you might hear. Another tale says that the date came to us from the Irish monks and grew out of early Celtic traditions. In the pagan Gaelic calendar, November 1 was the start of winter. The Druidic celebration of *Samhain* (remnants of which can still be seen in modern celebrations of Halloween) fell on the night before. *Samhain* was believed to be the night on which the door to the netherworld opened and the Lord of the Dead (*Donn*) called forth all the souls of the wicked people who had died during the past year.

The Church, in wisdom gained over the centuries, has often used pagan celebrations, sites, and traditions to explain Christian truths — as Boniface did with the Pantheon. Using this same wisdom to address the celebration of *Samhain*, the Irish monks took the pagan feast's focus on the dead and re-engineered it to focus on those living in heaven by setting the feast of All Saints on November 1. The vigil of the feast became known as All Hallows (as in "All Holy Saints") Eve, and was eventually shortened to the modern-day "Halloween."

Those Irish monks were also great missionaries. No doubt they realized that — at a time like the dark night of *Samhain* — stories about the saints could provide comforting images of eternal light and springtime in the cold countries of the Northern Hemisphere, wherever they travelled to spread the Gospel. As Pope John Paul II said in his encyclical on the laity, the "saints have always been the source and origin of renewal in the most difficult circumstances in the Church's history." [48]

The feast of All Souls (November 2) follows immediately after that of "All the Saints" and commemorates all the faithful departed — both those who are saints in heaven, but most especially those who are undergoing some final preparation, what we often call "purgation." The November 2 celebration is formally called "The Commemoration of All the Faithful Departed."

All Souls' Day as a feast dates at least to the Benedictine monasteries of the sixth century, when a feast to pray for the dead of the community was celebrated during the season of Pentecost. (Remember how Pentecost is the birthday of the Church and that the first Sunday after Pentecost was used to celebrate All Saints?) St. Odilo of Cluny (962–1049), around the year 1030, extended this practice to all the abbeys of his Benedictine order in France. But Odilo moved the day in memory of the faithful departed from the Pentecost season to November 2, since it followed All Saints Day. The feast spread across Europe and was adopted by the entire Western church around the thirteenth century. (In churches of the Eastern Catholic tradition, several days are set aside to remember and pray for the souls of the dead.)

The tradition of Catholic priests offering three requiem Masses on All Souls' Day can be traced to the Spanish Dominicans in the fifteenth century. This tradition spread through Spanish colonies and, after World War I, extended worldwide.

The Church teaches that the souls of the faithful departed are assured of heaven, but still need to be perfected in some way that will bring them to full and complete union with God through Christ. For this, they need our prayers. We do not completely understand how this perfection — formally called purgation — takes place, but the tradition of praying for the dead as they continue their final journey is very old in the Church.

In fact, one of the oldest teachings on prayer for the dead can be found in Jewish Scriptures, in the Second Book of Maccabees, written around the second century B.C. In it, Judas Maccabeus collects money to send to Jerusalem to be used to offer expiatory sacrifice for his dead soldiers. As the author notes, "if he were not expecting the fallen to rise again, it would have been superfluous and foolish to pray for the dead," but he had hope of them being "absolved from their sin" (2 Mc 12:44–45).

This reading, along with various New Testament writings such as Jesus' words about a final judgment (see Mt 25:31–46), helped teachers of the early Church (Ambrose, Jerome, Augustine, and others) develop the concept of what came to be called "purgatory."

At one time, people believed that souls in purgatory were malevolent — because they were suffering — and could return to haunt those who had wronged them in life, making them suffer as well. It was also believed that these souls could come back in many forms — especially as witches, black cats, and toads. Superstitious people, following those pagan traditions, believed that one could placate an angry soul with gifts, especially gifts of food. In other words, they could be prevented from playing tricks by the offering of treats. (Shades of modern Halloween.)

Today, we believe that the souls of the faithful departed are "our brothers and sisters who have gone to their rest in the hope of rising again" (Eucharistic Prayer II). We no longer believe that those undergoing purgation are suffering in agony, but rather that they are assured of the blessings of heaven and are at peace. While they remain in need of our prayers to reach that final glory, we are also in need of their prayers. Their work may be finished on earth, but — like the work of all those alive in Christ, including all the saints in heaven — it is not done.

Praying for the souls of the faithful departed at any time — and especially at the Mass on the feast of All Souls — helps them. When we pray for the dead, we are not praying for those who have reached heaven — since they are saints — or for those in hell, since they are eternally separated from God. Rather, we pray for those in "purgatory," those undergoing a cleansing transformation, that they might be freed from whatever keeps them from heaven. Church teaching on purgatory was largely set down by the Council of Trent (1563), though the idea of the need for a final purification has been with the Church since its earliest days.

In trying to understand purgatory, we need to stop and remember the purpose for which we were created: to seek God, to know Him, to share in the divine life, and to love God completely, as His own children. If we have not learned how to do this by the time we die, we will need to do so after death, through some form of purification — a purging of anything that keeps us from knowing and loving God completely. [49]

In Church history, there have been two general views on purgatory — largely paralleling the teachings of the Western and Eastern Catholic (and Eastern Orthodox) Churches. One teaching takes a legal view (Western), seeing purgatory as a way to balance the scales of justice. The other (Eastern), focuses on reaching a certain, final, and perfected relationship with God.

Traditionally, we in the Western Church have thought of purgatory as a place where we stay for a certain amount of time — sort of like fulfilling a legal sentence. But, as Pope John Paul II reminded us in a 1999 series of Angelus talks about "the final things," purgatory is more "a condition of existence" than a place or a time frame. The late pope explained that being ready for heaven is "a matter of loving God with all one's being, with purity of heart and the witness of deeds ... those who do not possess this integrity must undergo purification." [50]

However, while it's fairly easy to understand that the souls of the faithful departed need our prayers, we do not always as easily understand that these same souls can also pray for us. The Second Vatican Council reminded us of this truth in its document on the Church, better known as *Lumen Gentium*:

> All of us, however, in varying degrees and in different ways, share in the same charity towards God and our neighbors.... So it is that the union of the wayfarers with

those who sleep in the peace of Christ is in no way interrupted, but on the contrary, according to the constant faith of the Church, this union is reinforced by the exchange of spiritual goods." (No. 49)

We on earth and those who have died constantly take part in this "exchange of spiritual goods"; we pray for each other, and not just on the feast of All Souls. Every time we remember someone who has gone before us, we reach out in care to them and seek to bring them together with us and with all the saints in an ever closer union that is finally and fully realized only n heaven, in that glorious state of *Santo subito,* sainthood now. In praying for our departed loved ones, we're taking care of them — and they take care of us in return — just as we did when all of us shared the same space and time here on earth.

Discussion/Reflection:

1. How do you celebrate the feast of All Saints (November 1)? Of All Souls (November 2)?

2. When you pray for the dead, what do you most often ask for?

3. What was your first understanding of purgatory? Has that changed over the years?

CHAPTER THIRTEEN

The Past, the Present, and the Future

The Communion of Saints

Now we've come to the part where we can really get down to talking about that cheer of *Santo subito* — or "sainthood now" — not just for one saint, but for all of us. While we are here on earth, aspiring to be saints later on in heaven, we are all connected — at this very moment — to eternal sainthood. The connection comes through the "Communion of Saints," the *communio sanctorum.* This Latin phrase can be translated as either "the participation in holy or spiritual things" or as "the participation of holy ones."

The Second Vatican Council explained the Communion of Saints this way: "Some of His disciples are exiles on earth, some having died are being purified, and others are in glory beholding 'clearly God Himself triune and one, as He is,' but all in various ways and degrees are in communion in the same charity of God and neighbor and all sing the same hymn of glory to our God" (*Lumen Gentium*, No. 49).

So right now, this very moment, through this Communion of Saints, we are all sharing in the very same glory that the saints in heaven are experiencing. We all share *Santo subito* right now, just in different ways. These different ways of experiencing in the Communion of Saints even have their own titles.

Think of being back in school. You're in English class. The discussion has turned to verbs and their three major tenses: past, present, and future. The Church of Christ's Body could also be said to have three tenses — yet they all coexist at the very same time:

- The Church Suffering;

- The Church Militant; and

- The Church Triumphant.

These are not three *churches*, but three *states* of existence in the one Church that we call the Body of Christ. This Body, though many parts as St. Paul reminded us, is united in the Communion of Saints, the *communio sanctorum*.

The Catholic Church of the East reminds the faithful of this special union at each Eucharistic celebration (called the Divine Liturgy) by presenting the consecrated bread and wine with these words: "God's holy people sharing in God's holy things." As God's holy people, we *all* share in these holy things, the one glorious sacred Mystery, both now and in eternity. That sacred union includes *all* members of the Church — whether in the present, the past, or the future.

Present

Anyone reading this is a member of the *Church Militant* part of the Communion of Saints. We are the Church in the world — what the Second Vatican Council called "the pilgrim church." We experience the Body of Christ in time, in the present. We are active — militant — as in "engaged in serious matters," and, yes, even in a form of warfare in the sense that we are struggling. This title also reveals the work of the members of the Church Militant:

- We are meant to bring the Church into the world;

- We are meant to witness to Christ and to herald the Kingdom of God;

- We are meant to teach all nations and baptize them in the name of the Father, the Son, and the Holy Spirit.

Doing this, every day, year after year, is difficult. That difficulty and the constant need to persevere make the word "militant," with its soldierly context, seem apt.

"Christians, on pilgrimage toward the heavenly city," the Fathers of Vatican II said in the document on the Church in the Modern World, "should seek and think of these things which are above. This duty in no way decreases, rather it increases, the importance of their obligation to work with all people in the building of a more human world" (*Gaudium et Spes*, No. 57).

The Church Militant — the pilgrim church — is at work on earth. And God is at work in us. This is especially true in the sacraments, where we participate in the fruits of heaven and are strengthened for our work on earth. But it is also true in our prayers and in our ministry, no matter how humble. This is why we care for the poor and the weak here on earth, pray for the dead, and honor the saints. It is our work, our ministry now, and it is our commission in an army that marches on in a mission of love. We are militant in love, just as Christ was.

Past

Just as much as service for the living expresses the work of the Church Militant, so do prayers for the dead. Prayers for the dead are among the spiritual works of mercy. However, as we have seen, since we are all members of Christ's body and share in the Communion of Saints, our prayers for the dead are not a one-way street.

In the Communion of Saints, those who have died, but who have not yet reached the state of heaven, are known as "The Church Suffering" — for they are still struggling, though not in the same, active way as the Church Militant.

The Church Suffering has finished its work on earth — though there is still plenty of work for them to do. These are "our brothers and sisters [the faithful departed] who have gone to their rest in the hope of rising again" (Eucharistic Prayer II). Their work now involves undergoing a purification of some form — this is their "struggle." However, it is not the same as ours. Those who are being purified are still assured of heaven. They know that they will be with God, just as they know the saints already are. When their purification is done, they will be able to enter God's presence fully.

This is why the Church Suffering remains in need of our prayers — so that their purification will be finished and their joy become complete.

And we, the Church Militant, are also in need of their prayers. Their work on earth may be finished, but — like the work of all those in Christ's Body — it is not done. Instead, their work remains mysteriously linked to ours. And, since the faithful dead are linked to the saints and assured of heaven, their prayers for us are very beneficial.

The *Catechism of the Catholic Church* explains this link between the Church Militant and the Church Suffering as a sort of shared venture: "Our prayer for them is capable not only of helping them, but also of making their intercession for us effective" (CCC 958).

How can the prayers of those in purgatory help us? St. Robert Bellarmine (1542–1621), canonized in 1930 and made a Doctor of the Church a year later, explained that this happens because those in purgatory have *proven* their love for God, even if imperfectly and, because they are thus in union with Him, even though still imperfectly, their prayers have power to help us.

Because of this understanding of the true holiness of those who are in purgatory and of their assured future with God, another term for the Church Suffering is the "Church Expectant." Think of them as expectant parents, overjoyed with what is certain to come, even though they cannot partake in it completely yet. They can share, and want to share, their joy with us. And they do so in love.

Love is the essence of God, as the First Letter of John tells us. Divine, never-ending love is the link that connects all of us — whether we are in this life or the next.

Future

If the prayer of those who are still being perfected is powerful, how much more so is the prayer of those who are in perfect union with God now?

The saints are, clearly, part of the Communion of Saints. They are the future tense of the Church, traditionally called the "Church Triumphant." We know, of course, that their intercession for us is very powerful. As St. Thérèse of Lisieux promised on her deathbed (a promise miraculously confirmed by a shower of roses after her death), the saints desire to spend eternity doing good for those of us still on earth. They want to continue the mission of Christ, just as they did on earth, only in a new and more powerful way: think of it as a matter of different circumstances, but still the same work.

The Fathers of Vatican II said of the three states of the church:

> Until the Lord shall come in His majesty, and all the angels with Him and death being destroyed, all things are subject to Him; some of His disciples are exiles on earth,

some having died are purified, and others are in glory beholding "clearly God Himself triune and one, as He is," but all in various ways and degrees are in communion in the same charity of God and neighbor and all sing the same hymn of glory to our God. For all who are in Christ, having His Spirit, form one Church and cleave together in Him. (*Lumen Gentium*, No. 49)

There are three states, three ways of existence — past, present, and future — all working together in the one eternal Church, the Body of Christ. This Communion of Saints, of "holy people sharing holy things," exists exactly at the same time. *Santo subito,* "sainthood now," touches each of us because each of us is living in Christ — sharing in all three states — *right now,* just as the bishops of Vatican II said. It's a simple lesson told in three verbs, three states of being: militant, suffering (expectant), and triumphant. All, in their own ways, speak of what it means to be God's holy ones. We are all part of this wonderful Communion of Saints, assured that we share in, and cannot be separated from, Christ's love.

As Pope Paul VI said in 1968, "We believe in the communion of all the faithful of Christ, those who are pilgrims on earth, the dead who are attaining their purification, and the blessed in heaven, all together forming one church." [51]

That's a cause for cheering any day.

Discussion/Reflection:

1. How would you explain the Communion of Saints to a child? Would you use pictures or a song to help with the image?

2. Think about the three Churches: militant, suffering, and triumphant. Think up a new adjective for each of these three states of the one Church. Use words that have a powerful meaning in your life.

3. We often pray to the saints. Have you ever asked for help from the Holy Souls in purgatory?

CHAPTER FOURTEEN

"Yo-ho-ho!"

The Treasure Chest of the Church

Have you ever searched for buried treasure?

When I was little, we had lots of open fields around our house and a slough (marshy stream) nearby. Certain that lost treasure was scattered about out there, I spent a lot of time digging in the mud and searching rotten tree trunks. I gathered together a nice collection of pyrite (fool's gold), mica, and red granite. Once I even found an old library book. But no treasure.

The Church, however, has real treasure and it's kept in something called "the Treasury of the Church."

No, it's not located at the Vatican. It's not made up of gems or gold or even treasury bonds. It's definitely not hidden or buried anywhere.

Oh, yes, and "no moth or decay can destroy it."

Got it now?

Yes, the Treasury of the Church is located in Christ.

The *Catechism of the Catholic Church* explains this treasury as "the infinite value, which can never be exhausted, which Christ's merits have before God. They were offered so that the whole of mankind could be set free from sin and attain communion with the Father" (CCC 1476).

The Treasury of the Church is made of and sustained by the love with which Christ suffered for us in order to be able to open up to us an infinite supply of God's mercy. This treasury, through "the Keys of St. Peter," is now administered by the Church.

As Pope Clement VI wrote in the fourteenth century: "This treasure (Christ himself) is neither wrapped up in a napkin nor hid in a field, but entrusted to Blessed Peter, the keybearer, and his successors, that they might ... distribute it to the faithful in full or in partial remission for the temporal punishment due to sin." [52]

The pope (Peter's successor) generally makes distributions from the treasury by means of indulgences.

Indulgences have oftentimes been confusing — in fact, Martin Luther's 95 Theses (1517) spent a lot of time criticizing the practice of indulgences. And, to give Luther his due, at that time, indulgences were sometimes being sold for earthly treasure. Not so today. Much of the confusion today arises because we sometimes wonder why we would ever need anything beyond the absolution given to us in the sacrament of reconciliation.

Well, let's take a step back and look at the word "indulgent." We've all had someone in our past who was indulgent with us — maybe a grandmother or a grandpa, a favorite uncle, or a second grade teacher. They were generous with gifts, patient with our childish prattle, or just there for hugs when we fell down. Talk about an overflowing treasure chest.

Now remember: Our God is a loving and indulgent God. He showers us with grace and forgiveness. And He has given the Church — all of us with the bishops as our shepherds — ways to do the same for each other. One of these ways is indulgences. "Indulgence" comes from a Latin word *indulgeo*, meaning to be kind or tender.

Pope Paul VI, after the Second Vatican Council, issued an apostolic teaching on indulgences in 1967. In it, he explained indulgences as "the remission of the temporal punishment due for sins already forgiven insofar as their guilt is concerned." [53]

But wait a minute, someone reading this must be saying, "Didn't we just mention reconciliation and absolution? Isn't that sacrament all about the forgiveness of sins? With absolution, sins are washed away, right? What's with this 'temporal punishment' thing?"

You're right. Absolution grants forgiveness of sins — it takes away guilt, as Pope Paul said. That's why the sacrament is called "reconciliation"; our sins are washed away and we are reunited with God and with each other.

However, there are consequences for every action, and sin is no different. While we are indeed reconciled through the sacrament, there is still the matter of justice and restitution. Don't think of it as punishment. Think of it in terms of repairs needed after an accident. Even if we say we're sorry about a broken window and we are forgiven, the window still needs fixing. Someone has to pay for it.

That payment for a window serves as an analogy for what we call the "temporal remission of sins." Pope Paul went on to explain that every sin "causes a perturbation in the universal order established by God...." Things get messed up by sin. Pope Paul added that it is "therefore necessary, for the full remission and — as it is called— reparation of sins, not only that friendship with God be reestablished ... but also that all the personal as well as social values and those of the universal order itself, which have been diminished or destroyed by sin, be fully reintegrated." [54]

Yes, we have forgiveness of sins. Our friendship with God is reestablished through the sacrament of reconciliation. However, in ways we cannot begin to understand, the effects of sin still remain even after our sins are forgiven. This is because our God is a just God, as well as a loving and forgiving God. So we also have indulgences.

As *The Catholic Encyclopedia* explains, after reconciliation something called "temporal punishment" is still "required by divine justice, and this requirement must be fulfilled either in the present life or in the world to come.... An indulgence offers the penitent sinner the means of discharging this debt during his life on earth." [55] We have to, as Pope Paul VI explained, make amends for our offense: order on a universal scale (remember the Communion of Saints thing?) must be "fully integrated." (This, of course, is what is happening with those who are in purgatory.)

Now, it's too complicated to try to go into how this is done, or what "temporal punishment" entails and what "fully integrated" mean. Books have been written on this. However, just keep that broken window in mind. It has to be repaired. The idea of indulgences, God's justice, and "temporal punishment" all fit into the same allegory. Something needs to be fixed. Someone has to pay for it. That payment brings us back to the Treasury of the Church.

The main point to remember is that the treasury is there to fix things. It's never going to run empty, no matter how many windows we break; Christ's self-giving love on the Cross filled it up for all time; Christ's love did everything that was ever needed to make everything eternally right; Jesus Christ set us free; His death washed us clean of our sins and set up for us an unending treasure of love to keep us free from sin for eternity. This is why we call it the "Treasury of the Church."

However, even though the Treasury of the Church will never run out, our loving God gave us a chance to add to it. This is what St. Paul meant when he wrote to the Colossians, "I am filling up what is lacking in the afflictions of Christ on behalf of his body, which is the church" (1:24).

Now, we just said the Treasury of the Church could never — would never — ever run out. Christ's contribution to it was more than enough; it was perfect. Nothing more is needed. So how could Paul talk about "filling up what was lacking" in the treasury?

By the grace of God, Paul — through his sufferings, ministry, and prayers — realized that he was able to add to the treasury. Not because the treasury needed it, but because *Paul* needed it. It's a mystery, but God's mercy allows us to share in what Christ perfectly did.

The Catholic Encyclopedia calls what we put into the treasury "a secondary deposit, not independent of, but rather acquired through, the merits of Christ." [56] These secondary deposits can be made in many ways: we can make them through prayers for other people, good deeds, self-denials, and even our sufferings when we link them to those of Christ. All these can become part of the treasury, more jewels set right alongside those of Christ. These secondary deposits then become part of a treasure that belongs to the loving union we call the "Communion of Saints." As we said earlier, in that communion we are all — whether living here or living after our life on earth — present to one another and able to help one another through Christ.

That treasury of love with which Christ suffered for us in order to open for us the infinite supply of God's mercy, and to which He has graciously allowed us to share in increasing, is something we all have access to through the Church. Administered by the Church under the guidance of the popes, the treasury can be accessed in several ways, including:

- the prayers of the Church,
- the celebration of the Mass, and
- indulgences.

Here we are, back at indulgences. Pope Paul VI explained how it works, at least on our end: "In an indulgence, in fact, the Church, making use of its power as minister of the Redemption of Christ, not only prays, but, by an authoritative intervention, dispenses to the faithful suitably disposed the treasury of satisfaction which Christ and the saints won for the remission of temporal punishment." [57]

Remembering the confusion of the time of the Protestant Reformation, we might cringe a little when we hear anything about indulgences. But we shouldn't. Just think of indulgences as one way of opening the treasure chest. Peter received the keys, didn't he?

Those keys can open the treasure chest to dispense both partial and full indulgences.

Certain prayers or devotions traditionally have partial indulgences attached to them. At one time, these were indicated as being a certain number of days' release from purgatory. However, since purgatory, as we already explored, is not a place or time, but a state of being, we need to think of this "release" in terms of being freed from whatever need of purification would have resulted from our transgression. Pope Paul himself removed any "time equivalencies" from partial indulgences.

A plenary indulgence is used more infrequently than a partial indulgence because it is also more encompassing. Pope Benedict XVI allowed plenary indulgences during the Year of Faith in 2012–2013 and Pope Francis issued one for World Youth Day in 2013. One was also granted to everyone who received the first blessing of Pope Francis on March 13, 2013.

When you hear "plenary," just think of "more than enough," or of "plenty." A plenary indulgence completely "frees someone from any temporal punishment due for sins" (canon 993). It can be applied either to one's self or offered for a deceased person to help them through their own period of purgation. Here we again see the interactions of the Church Militant with the Church Suffering (Expectant) in the Communion of Saints. We're sharing the treasure chest — sort of a "yo-ho-ho" moment all around. (For the requirements to receive a plenary indulgence, see Appendix II.)

A plenary indulgence may be a rare thing, just like a jewel found in a treasure chest is rare. However, jewels from the Treasury of the Church are more lasting than any ruby or sapphire, and they come from a loving and generous God who so wants us to share in the divine life that He allows our small offerings to become as precious as Christ's. As St. Athanasius wrote in the fourth century, "God became man that we might become like God." God is love and, through the Treasury of the Church, God allows us not only to profit from that merciful love but to become an active part of it.

If I were to look at it from a child's eyes, I would say that we didn't make the treasure; we didn't make the gems; we didn't mine them; we didn't even bring them anywhere in a wooden chest, or build the wooden chest itself. Still, like a gem-cutter or a merchant, through the Communion of Saints, we can use our own small efforts to take that treasure and shape it, polish it, and offer it in such a way as to reveal the shining and glorious fire that lies at its heart — because the heart of that treasury is the priceless love of God revealed in Christ, and it's inexhaustible.

Discussion/Reflection:

1. Have you ever "offered it up?" What have you offered up? Did you realize you were adding to the Treasury of the Church?

2. What image would you use to describe the Treasury of the Church?

3. What do you think about indulgences? Does the concept of an indulgence give you comfort or does it upset or confuse you?

CHAPTER FIFTEEN

Seeing God Face to Face

The Beatific Vision

In our modern world, social networking, voice mail, video conferencing, and cell phones can make communication instantaneous and worldwide. Yet the best form of communication remains the face to face kind. When we are with someone, we will be able to communicate the most directly — using voice, expression, gesture, inflection, and even touch. It's the closest we can get to another. In this life, anyway.

What about the next life?

The Church teaches that we are subject to the judgment of God when this life ends. Yes, there is something that we call the Final Judgment, which will take place at the Second Coming of Christ. However, there is also the Particular Judgment. The *Catechism of the Catholic Church* explains this as "each will be rewarded immediately after death in accordance with his works and faith" (CCC 1021). It then goes on to remind us of Christ's word to the dying thief on the Cross: "Today you will be with me in Paradise" (Lk 23:43).

Sort of sounds like the Lord was saying *Santo subito* — "Make him a saint now!" — doesn't it?

In that Particular Judgment, when we come face to face with God, that's what we all hope to hear: "You will be with me in Paradise." When the Church beatifies an individual, declaring him or her "blessed," this is what it essentially means: that we believe that this person has been so blessed as to behold God directly, face to face, and hear His voice.

In the Sermon on the Mount, Jesus promised the "clean of heart" that they would see God (Matthew 5:8). This is one of the Scripture texts from which we derive the concept of the beatific vision, of "being in heaven." The beatific vision — also called "the intuitive vision" — means seeing God face to face. In 1336, Pope Benedict XII set down clearly the teaching on the beatific vision: "these souls have seen and see the divine essence with an intuitive vision and even face to face, without the mediation of any creature clearly and openly...." [58]

Paul, in the First Letter to the Corinthians, written about twenty years after Christ's resurrection, put it in more picturesque terms: "At present we see indistinctly, as in a mirror, but then face to face" (1 Corinthians 13:12). And the First Letter of John states plainly that "we shall see him as he is" (3:2).

But what does it mean to see God "as He is?"

The *Catechism of the Catholic Church* says, "The beatific vision, in which God opens himself in an inexhaustible way to the elect, will be the ever-flowing wellspring of happiness, peace and mutual communion" (CCC 1045).

That's heaven. Happiness, peace, and face to face communion. It's been our destiny from the very beginning: To know God, to love God, and to serve God, and be happy with God forever. (*Baltimore Catechism*, Lesson One.)

Yet admit it, don't you have some doubts about how fun this all might be? Doesn't our concept of heaven, of being eternally happy and at peace (not to mention sitting on clouds and playing harps), seem a bit static?

"Too often," said the late Jesuit Cardinal Avery Dulles, "eternal life has been depicted as a kind of lonely contemplation. It is as though each beatified soul were in a box of a theater, equipped with a pair of opera glasses, sharply focused on the divine essence, but totally oblivious to the persons sitting in the adjacent seats." [59]

Yet experiencing the beatific vision, being in union with God, can hardly be like watching a play, can it? God, our creator and sustainer, the one who loves us so much that He sent His Son to die for us, can hardly plan to be as distant to us in eternity as an actor standing before an audience.

No, Christ's life on earth assures us that God graciously seeks direct union — with each one of us and with all of us together — through Christ, in a way that is sustained by the Holy Spirit. The God who so wished to communicate this with us that He sent his Son to become one of us and live among us could hardly be content with anything as distant as a stage performance.

At the very least, we should think of being in heaven as being part of that great Divine play as well. Not out there in the audience, but right up there with the stage lights and interacting intimately with God.

"The concept of beatific vision is best understood if we think of it in terms of a living, personal exchange between God and the human person," explained Franciscan spiritual writer Fr. Zachary Hayes. "God offers the mystery of the divine presence to the creature. The human person, on the other hand, is freed from self-seeking and stands before God in total openness." [60]

Total openness hardly means that we'll be watching from the audience. Total openness means that the beatific vision is not just about seeing God, but about being seen with God and by God and about seeing ourselves just as God sees us. As Paul said, "Then I shall know fully, as I am fully known" (1 Corinthians 13:12).

Archbishop Daniel Pilarczyk, retired president of the National Conference of Catholic Bishops and retired Archbishop of Cincinnati, explained this knowledge of ourselves, seeing ourselves as God sees us, as true fulfillment. And this should be a comfort when we think back, at the end of life, on all the things we didn't do before the end drew near.

"The potential that God created for each of us will not be lost," Archbishop Pilarczyk wrote, "but will be actualized and brought to terms in the glorious humanity of Christ. Our capacity for loving and being loved, for intellectual achievement, for appreciating God's works, and for communicating with others, the things we might have been but never got the chance to be, the things we started but never got the chance to finish — all will be brought to completion in the life of Father, Son, and Holy Spirit manifested in us." [61]

Now that's a beautiful and freeing vision. And it shows us that how we will share in God's life will mean being anything *but* static. As St. Thérèse of Lisieux promised — a promise verified by that shower of roses after her death — "I shall spend my heaven doing good on earth." (There's that Communion of Saints coming into play again!)

With the promise of a dynamic and interactive beatific vision awaiting us, we can strive *now* to better know Christ, who is "God with Us." Through Him, we can draw ever closer to that perfect communication which the beatified and the saints in heaven now fully share — with God and with all who live in God. With that vision in mind, we can actually start to live *Santo subito* — sainthood now! — this very day.

Striving to live as Jesus did on earth, with the saints as examples and the treasury of Christ's love and the Communion of Saints to sustain us, can help us join — however dimly — in that perfect sharing that is heaven. The saints — now alive with God — help weave us into that perfect sharing. When we do as they did when they were on earth — make peace, seek righteousness, show mercy — we are taking part in the best form of communication ever: love revealed through — and taught face to face by — Christ.

Pope Paul VI, whose sainthood cause is being explored by the Vatican, wrote the following for an Angelus message on the feast of the Transfiguration of Christ (August 6) in 1978:

> On top of Mount Tabor, for a few moments, Christ raises the veil which hides the resplendence of his divinity, and he is manifested to the chosen witnesses as he really is, the Son of God — "the splendor of the glory of the Father and the image of his substance" (Hebrews 1:5); but at the same time He reveals the transcendent destiny of our human nature which He has taken on in order to save us, destined as it is (by having been redeemed by his sacrifice of irrevocable love) to participate in the fullness of life, in the "inheritance of the saints in light" (Colossians 1:12).
>
> That body, which is transfigured before the astonished eyes of the Apostles, is the body of Christ our brother, but it is also our body destined for the glory; the light which inundates it is, and will also be, our part of the inheritance and the splendor. [62]

Isn't that a wonderful promise? And a great insight. Our bodies are destined for glory. The pope himself, however, never delivered this message in person; he died that same day and, as we believe, instantly met God face to face.

Think of the wonder. Think of the beauty and the love. To share at once in Christ's glory. To know what we pray for now: to hear, at the moment of death, these words from our loving Lord: "*Santo subito*: Make him, make her, a saint now."

Discussion/Reflection:

1. What do you think God will be like when you see God face to face? How is that image different for you today than when you were 5 years old? When you were 15 years old?

2. What experiences in earthly life do you think give us a hint of what the beatific vision might be like?

3. Why do you believe in heaven?

4. Repetitive prayer can be very insightful because it frees up the imagination. Take a moment or two right now to close your eyes, settle your breathing, and prayerfully repeat: "*Santo subito*, sainthood now, *Santo subito*, sainthood now…." What images come into your heart? What new words might want to fit themselves into the repetition? Is there a hint of music? Do you feel the saints as they join you in your prayer? Where is God for you, at this moment?

Appendix I

Doctors of the Church

Ambrose (c. 340–397). Bishop of Milan, Italy. Named a Doctor of the Church: 1298.

Jerome (c. 343–420). Using Hebrew and Greek sources, compiled into Latin much of the Old and New Testaments and gave us the version of the Bible known as the *Vulgate*. Named a Doctor of the Church: 1298.

Augustine of Hippo (c. 354–430). Bishop of Hippo (North Africa). Wrote *Confessions* and *City of God*. Called the "Doctor of Grace" (*Doctor Gratiae*). Named a Doctor of the Church: 1298.

Gregory the Great (I) (c. 540–604). Pope. Named a Doctor of the Church: 1298.

Basil the Great (c. 329–379). Bishop of Caesarea (Asia Minor). Named a Doctor of the Church: 1568.

Gregory of Nazianzus (c. 330–390), Bishop of Constantinople (now Turkey). Named a Doctor of the Church: 1568.

John Chrysostom ("Golden-Mouthed") (c. 347–407). Archbishop of Constantinople. Named a Doctor of the Church: 1568.

Athanasius (c. 297–373). Bishop of Alexandria (Egypt). Named a Doctor of the Church: 1568.

Thomas Aquinas (1225–1274). Italian Dominican. Wrote *Summa Theologica*. Called the "Angelic Doctor" (*Doctor Angelicus*). Named a Doctor of the Church: 1568.

Bonaventure (c. 1217–1274). Franciscan Bishop of Albano (Italy). Called the "Seraphic Doctor" (*Doctor Seraphicus*). Named a Doctor of the Church: 1588.

Anselm of Canterbury (1033–1109). Archbishop. Called the "Magnificent Doctor" (*Doctor Magnificus*). Named a Doctor of the Church: 1720.

Isidore of Seville (c. 560–636). Bishop of Seville (Spain). Named a Doctor of the Church: 1722.

Peter Chrysologus ("Gold-Worded") (c. 400–450). Archbishop of Ravenna, Italy. Named a Doctor of the Church: 1729.

Leo (I) the Great (c. 400–461). Pope. Named a Doctor of the Church: 1754.

Peter Damian (1007–1072). Italian Benedictine and cardinal. Named a Doctor of the Church: 1828.

Bernard of Clairvaux (c. 1090–1153). French Cistercian abbot. Called the "Mellifluous Doctor" ("Honey-voiced"). Named a Doctor of the Church: 1830.

Hilary of Poitiers (c. 315–368), Bishop of Poitiers (France). Named a Doctor of the Church: 1851.

Alphonsus Liguori (1696–1787). Founder of Redemptorists. Called the "Doctor Most Zealous" (*Doctor Zelantissimus*). Named a Doctor of the Church: 1871.

Francis de Sales (1567–1622). Bishop of Geneva (Switzerland). Patron of Catholic writers and press. Called the "Doctor of Charity" (*Doctor Caritatas*). Named a Doctor of the Church: 1877.

Cyril of Alexandria (c. 376–444). Bishop. Doctor of the Incarnation (*Doctor Incarnationis*). Named a Doctor of the Church: 1882.

Cyril of Jerusalem (c. 315–386). Bishop. Named a Doctor of the Church: 1882.

John Damascene (c. 675–749). Syrian monk. Called *Chrysoarhhoas* ("Golden Speaker"). Named a Doctor of the Church: 1890.

Bede the Venerable (c. 673–735). English Benedictine. The "Father of English History." Named a Doctor of the Church: 1899.

Ephrem the Syrian (c. 306–373). Deacon and poet. Named a Doctor of the Church: 1920.

Peter Canisius (1521–1597). Dutch Jesuit and catechist. Named a Doctor of the Church: 1925.

John of the Cross (1542–1591). Founder of Discalced Carmelites. Called the "Mystic Doctor" (*Doctor Mysticus*). Named a Doctor of the Church: 1926.

Robert Bellarmine (1542–1621). Italian Jesuit, archbishop of Capua (Italy). Wrote Reformation-era doctrine defenses and catechisms. Named a Doctor of the Church: 1931.

Albert the Great (or Magnus) (c. 1200–1280). German Dominican, bishop of Regensburg. Called the "Universal Doctor" (*Doctor Universalis*). Named a Doctor of the Church: 1931.

Anthony of Padua (1195–1231). Franciscan preacher. Called the "Evangelic Doctor" (*Doctor Evangelicus*). Named a Doctor of the Church: 1946.

Lawrence of Brindisi (1559–1619). Italian Capuchin Franciscan. Called the "Apostolic Doctor" (*Doctor Apostolicus*). Named a Doctor of the Church: 1959.

Catherine of Siena (c. 1347–1380). Italian Third Order Dominican, mystical author. Named a Doctor of the Church: 1970.

Teresa of Ávila (1515–1582). Spanish Carmelite, initiated discalced Carmelite movement. First woman Doctor of the Church. Named a Doctor of the Church: 1970.

Thérèse of Lisieux (1873–1897). French Carmelite, wrote spiritual autobiography. Called the "Doctor of Love" (*Doctor Amorius*). Named a Doctor of the Church: 1997.

John of Ávila (1500–1569). Spanish priest and mystic. Named a Doctor of the Church: 2012

Hildegard of Bingen (1098–1179). German abbess, composer, and mystic. Known as the Sibyl of the Rhine. Named a Doctor of the Church: 2012.

Appendix II

Plenary Indulgences

A plenary (complete) indulgence completely "frees someone from any temporal punishment due for sins" (canon 993). It can be applied either to oneself or offered for a deceased person to help them through their own period of purgation.

There are requirements to earn a plenary indulgence granted by the Holy Father. Pope Paul VI set down the norms in 1967 (*Indulgentiarum Doctrina*, "Apostolic Constitution On Indulgences"). One seeking a plenary indulgence must do the following:

- Perform the specific work to which the indulgence has been attached by the pope, such as a pilgrimage (for example, attending World Youth Day);
- Make a sacramental confession;
- Receive Eucharistic Communion;
- Pray for the intentions of the pope.

The last three conditions must be fulfilled "several days before or after" performing the first. Only one indulgence may be received per day. A single confession is sufficient to receive several plenary indulgences, but receiving Communion and praying for the papal intentions must be done for each indulgence sought.

Pope Paul also added a final requirement: "That all attachment to sin, even to venial sin, be absent. If this disposition is in any way less than complete, or if the prescribed three conditions are not fulfilled, the indulgence will be only partial."

Notes

Chapter One

1. Paul Molinari, S.J., The Catholic University of America, "Canonization of Saints," *New Catholic Encyclopedia* (New York: McGraw-Hill, 1967), Vol. 3.

2. Thomas Malcolm Muggeridge, *Something Beautiful for God* (New York: Harper and Row Publishers, Inc., 1971).

3. Ibid.

4. Address of Pope John Paul II to the Pilgrims Who Had Come to Rome for the Beatification of Mother Teresa, No. 2, October 20, 2003. Retrieved from www.vatican.va/holy_father/john_paul_ii/speeches/2003/october/doc uments/hf_jp-ii_spe_20031020_pilgrims-mother-teresa_en.html on August 4, 2012.

5. T.N. Jagadisan, *Mahatma Gandhi Answers the Challenge of Leprosy*, Madras, 1965.

6. Ann Schneible, ZENIT News, April 30, 2011. Retrieved from www .zenit.org/en/articles/world-celebrates-beatification-of-john-paul-ii-a-year-later on June 13, 2013. Used with permission.

7. Archbishop Fulton J. Sheen, *Go To Heaven* (New York: McGraw Hill, 1960).

Chapter Two

8. C. Beccari (1908), "Confessor," *The Catholic Encyclopedia* (New York: Robert Appleton Company). Retrieved from New Advent www.newad vent.org/cathen/04215a.htm on August 3, 2012.

9. Dennis Sweetland, "Disciple," *The Modern Catholic Encyclopedia* (St. Cloud, Minn.: A Michael Glazier Book by Liturgical Press, 1994).

Chapter Three

10. Fr. Thomas A Kleissler, Margo C. LeBert, and Mary A. McGuinnes, *Renewing for the 21st Century*, RENEW International, Season I, 1998, and *Small Christian Communities: A Vision of Hope in the 21st Century*, 1997

(revised 2003). Reprinted with permission from RENEW International, Plainfield, N.J.

11. H. Ford (1907), "St. Benedict of Nursia," *The Catholic Encyclopedia* (New York: Robert Appleton Company). Retrieved from New Advent www .newadvent.org/cathen/02467b.htm on August 9, 2012.

12. Pope Benedict XVI, General Audience, April 9, 2008. Retrieved on August 9, 2012 from www.vatican.va/holy_father/benedict_xvi/audi ences/2008/documents/hf_ben-xvi_aud_20080409_en.html.

13. Pope Paul VI, *Pacis Nuntius* ("Messenger of Peace"), October 24, 1964. Retrieved August 9, 2012 from www.vatican.va/holy_father/paul_vi/ apost_letters/documents/hf_p-vi_apl_19641024_pacis-nuntius_it.html.

14. *The Rule of St. Benedict.* Retrieved from Medieval Sourcebook at Fordham University www.fordham.edu/halsall/source/rul-benedict.asp on August 9, 2012.

Chapter Four

15. H. Thurston (1911), "Relics," *The Catholic Encyclopedia* (New York: Robert Appleton Company). Retrieved from New Advent www.newad vent.org/cathen/12734a.htm on August 10, 2012.

16. Norman P. Tanner, ed., *Decrees of the Ecumenical Councils, Vol. 1* (Washington, D.C .: Georgetown University Press, 1990).

17. *General Instruction of the Roman Missal* (Washington, D.C.: United States Catholic Conference, 2003), No. 302.

18. St. Thomas Aquinas. *Summa Theologica*, Part III, Question 26, Article 5. Retrieved from New Advent www.newadvent.org on June 13, 2013.

19. H. Thurston (1911), "Relics," *The Catholic Encyclopedia* (New York: Robert Appleton Company). Retrieved from New Advent www.newad vent.org/cathen/12734a.htm on August 10, 2012.

20. Dana C. Munro, "The Fourth Crusade" *Translations and Reprints from the Original Sources of European History* (Philadelphia: University of Pennsylvania, [n.d.] 189?), Vol 3:1, 1-18. Retrieved from the Internet Medieval Sourcebook at Fordhum University www.fordham.edu/halsall/sbook .asp on June 13, 2013.

21. *On the Invocation, Veneration, and Relics of Saints and on Sacred Images.* The Council of Trent, second decree. Retrieved from www.thecouncil oftrent.com/ch25.htm on June 13, 2013.

22. St. Thomas Aquinas. *Summa Theologica*, Part III, Question 26, Article 5. Retrieved from New Advent www.newadvent.org on June 13, 2013.

Chapter Five

23. C. Beccari (1907), "Beatification and Canonization," *The Catholic Encyclopedia* (New York: Robert Appleton Company). Retrieved from New Advent www.newadvent.org/cathen/02364b.htm on June 14, 2013.

24. *The Fourth Lateran Council*, 1215. Electronic text retrieved from the Internet Medieval Sourcebook website at history.hanover.edu/courses/ excerpts/344lat.html on Aug 18, 2012.

25. John Calvin, *A Treatise on Relics* (Edinburgh: Johnstone and Hunter, 1543).

Chapter Six

26. Pope John Paul II, *Divinus Perfectionis Magister*, Chapter I:1. January 25, 1983. Retrieved from Vatican website www.vatican.va on June 14, 2013.

27. Congregation for the Causes of Saints, *New Laws for the Causes of Saints*, No. 9, 1983. Retrieved from Vatican website www.vatican.va on June 13, 2013.

28. Cindy Wooden, "Pope receives papers for cause of Archbishop Sheen, whom he knew," May 25, 2011, Catholic News Service, Washington, D.C. Retrieved from www.catholicnews.com/data/stories/cns/1102062.htm on June 13, 2013. Used with permission.

29. Bruno Chenu, *The Book of Christian Martyrs* (London: SCM Press, 1988).

30. "French nun says life has changed since she was healed thanks to JPII," March 30, 2007, Catholic News Service, Washington, D.C. Retrieved from www.catholicnews.com/data/stories/cns/0701771.htm on June 13, 2013. Used with permission.

31. "Pope Francis signs canonization decrees for John XXIII and John Paul II," Vatican Radio, July 5, 2013. Retrieved from www.news.va/en/news/pope-francis-signs-canonization-decrees-for-john-x.

Chapter Seven

32. *The Roman Missal*, Third Typical Edition, No. 39 (Chicago, Ill.: Archdiocese of Chicago, Liturgical Training Publications, 2011).

33. Alberto Valentini, "Birth of Mary," *Dictionary of Mary* (New York: Catholic Book Publishing Company, 1985).

34. Liturgy of the Hours, Office of Readings, September 8. Retrieved from www.ebriviary.com on June 13, 2013.

35. C.C. Martindale (1908), "Christmas," *The Catholic Encyclopedia* (New York: Robert Appleton Company). Retrieved from New Advent www.newadvent.org/cathen/03724b.htm on June 14, 2013.

36. The Order of St. Benedict, *Days of the Lord: the Liturgical Year: Volume I: Advent, Christmas, Epiphany* (Collegeville, Minn., 1991).

Chapter Eight

37. H. Thurston (1911), "Christian Names," *The Catholic Encyclopedia* (New York: Robert Appleton Company). Retrieved from New Advent www.newadvent.org/cathen/10673c.htm on June 15, 2013.

38. Maria Augusta Trapp, *Around the Year with the Trapp Family* (New York: Pantheon Books, Inc., 1955).

39. Maria Faustina Kowalska, *Divine Mercy in My Soul* (Stockbridge, Mass.: Congregation of Marians of the Immaculate Conception, 1987), p. 360.

Chapter Nine

40. Pope Paul VI, *Indulgentiarum Doctrina*, No. 5, January 1, 1967. Retrieved from Vatican website www.vatican.va/holy_father/paul_vi/apost_constitutions/documents/hf_p-vi_apc_19670101_indulgentiarum-doctrina_en.html on June 13, 2013.

Chapter Ten

41. Pope Paul VI, Homily, October 4, 1970. Retrieved from Vatican website www.vatican.va on June 15, 2013.

42. Pope John Paul II, Homily, October 19, 1997. Retrieved from Vatican website www.vatican.va on June 15, 2013.

43. Pope John Paul II, *Mulieris dignitatem* ("On the Dignity and Vocation of Women"), August 15, 1988. Retrieved from Vatican website www .vatican.va on June 15, 2013.

44. Pope Benedict XVI, General Audience, September 1, 2010. Retrieved from Vatican website www.vatican.va on June 15, 2013.

Chapter Eleven

45. John Calvin, *Institutes of the Christian Religion*, Book One, Chapter 11 (1536). Retrieved from Christian Classics Ethereal Library at www.ccel .org on June 14, 2013.

46. Martin Luther, *The Large Catechism*, trans. F. Bente and W. H. T. Dau, Penn State Electronic Classics edition. Retrieved from www2.hn.psu .edu/faculty/jmanis/m-luther/mllc.pdf on June 15, 2013.

47. Ibid.

Chapter Twelve

48. Pope John Paul II, *Christifideles Laici* ("On the Vocation and the Mission of the Lay Faithful"), December 30, 1988. Retrieved from Vatican website www.vatican.va on June 15, 2013.

49. See *Catechism of the Catholic Church*, paragraph 1.

50. Pope John Paul II, General Audience, August 4, 1999. Retrieved from Vatican website www.vatican.va on June 15, 2013.

Chapter Thirteen

51. Pope Paul VI, *Credo of the People of God*, June 30, 1968. Retrieved from Vatican website www.vatican.va on June 15, 2013.

Chapter Fourteen

52. W. Kent (1910), "Indulgences," *The Catholic Encyclopedia* (New York: Robert Appleton Company). Retrieved from New Advent www .newadvent.org/cathen/07783a.htm on June 15, 2013.

53. Pope Paul VI, *Indulgentiarum Doctrina*, No. 8, January 1, 1967. Retrieved from Vatican website www.vatican.va/holy_father/paul_vi/ apost_constitutions/documents/hf_p-vi_apc_19670101_indulgentiarum-doctrina_en.html on June 13, 2013.

54. Ibid., No. 3.

55. W. Kent (1910), "Indulgences," *The Catholic Encyclopedia* (New York: Robert Appleton Company). Retrieved from New Advent www .newadvent.org/cathen/07783a.htm on June 15, 2013.

56. Ibid.

57. Pope Paul VI, *Indulgentiarum Doctrina*, No. 8, January 1, 1967. Retrieved from Vatican website www.vatican.va/holy_father/paul_vi/ apost_constitutions/documents/hf_p-vi_apc_19670101_indulgentiarum-doctrina_en.html on June 13, 2013.

Chapter Fifteen

58. Pope Benedict XII, *Benedictus Deus* (On the Beatific Vision of God), 1336. Retrieved from Papal Encyclicals Online www.papalencyclicals.net/ Ben12/B12bdeus.html on June 13, 2013.

59. Avery Dulles, *The Craft of Theology: From Symbol to System* (New York: The Crossroad Publishing Company, March 1995, first ed. April 1992).

60. Fr. Zachary Hayes, O.F.M., "Beatific Vision," *The New Dictionary of Theology* (Collegeville, Minn.: A Michael Glazier Book by Liturgical Press, 1987).

61. Archbishop Daniel Pilarczyk, *We Believe: Essentials of Catholic Faith*. (Cincinnati: St. Anthony Messenger Press, 1990).

62. Pope Paul VI, Angelus, August 6, 1978. Retrieved in Spanish on May 3, 2013, from www.vatican.va/holy_father/paul_vi/angelus/1978/ documents/hf_p-vi_ang_19780806_sp.html. English translation by Sister Maria Drzewiecki, O.S.F.